Why This B for the American People

"It would be an understatement to say that I am shocked and somewhat appalled at how our nation's education reform movement is impacting our schools and communities today. Since I haven't been in a public school classroom for several decades, I had no idea how much stress and pressure is being placed upon our students and their teachers. This book has opened my eyes to what is going on and serves as a wake-up call for the American people."

Nina Keck, grandmother and concerned citizen
Green Valley, Arizona

"On behalf of our nation's teachers, I sincerely appreciate the deep understanding and personal respect that Corky gives to our profession in this important book. Teachers have been working in a pressure cooker for a number of years. Today, with the implementation of the Common Core Standards on the line, many of us are feeling overwhelmed and undervalued."

Karen Muldowney, mother and devoted teacher
West Bend, Wisconsin

"In thanking my friend Corky for writing this book, I speak for many other superintendents throughout our country. He has done what we all must do. He has created for the American people an honest portrayal of the true state of our nation's public schools and then challenged them to get involved in helping shape the future of education reform."

Mike Paskewicz, Superintendent of Schools
Northview Public Schools, Grand Rapids, Michigan

"This book is a must-read for anyone who wants to learn the truth about how the education reform movement in our country is impacting our students, teachers, and taxpayers and what they can do about it. It is an excellent companion piece to the educational documentary, *Rise Above the Mark.*

> Rocky Killion, Superintendent of Schools
> West Lafayette School Corporation, West Lafayette,
> Indiana, and Indiana's 2015 Superintendent of the Year

"This is exactly the message that the public at large needs to hear about what has happened and is happening to our schools."

> Tracey DeBruyn, CEO
> The Master Teacher, Inc., Manhattan, Kansas

"All Americans—with and without children in school—must participate in a conversation regarding the future of our public schools. Corky's book, which draws on years of experience, serves as an excellent starting point."

> Jamie Vollmer, nationally known speaker
> and author of *Schools Cannot Do It Alone*

America's Schools at a Turning Point

And how we THE PEOPLE can help shape their future

Corky O'Callaghan

America's Schools at a Turning Point:
And how we THE PEOPLE can help shape their future

Published by Wheatmark®
1760 East River Road, Suite 145, Tucson, Arizona 85718 USA
www.wheatmark.com

Author photo by Skip Bangs

ISBN: 978-1-62787-198-3 (paperback)
ISBN: 978-1-62787-199-0 (ebook)
LCCN: 2014951572

This book is dedicated to the millions of Americans
who believe in our country and want to make a difference.

Contents

Part III
Missing from Our National Discussion, 97

Part IV
Reason for Hope, 127

Part V
Where We Go from Here, 165

Foreword

"Seek first to understand, then to be understood." That quote from Stephen Covey was his first advice to a new school superintendent who was about to embark on an uncertain journey with his community. His constant admonition to "really listen in order to deeply understand and learn" enabled the new superintendent to help his school district and community achieve some pretty amazing things.

I was that superintendent, and for thirteen years the author of this book was there for me. It should be noted that I will refer to him as Corky rather than William, not just because he has become one of my closest friends and continues to be a colleague, but because that is what everyone who knows him calls him.

Corky challenged my thinking—and still does—as he continually pushed me to reflect more deeply upon what was really important. At the same time, he was learning with me. He never pretended to have all of the answers and wouldn't hesitate to ask the often difficult questions, including, "Are you truly listening to the community?" and "What are you learning?"

From his journey helping scores of school leaders find ways to strengthen the bond between their schools and communities, Corky has become a voracious learner who believes that what matters most is hard work and trust between people who genuinely care for one another. Paradoxically, many of those who have come to rely on him have been his teachers. His humility, common sense, and passion define who he is.

Corky's stories are anything but today's norm. He doesn't promote magical processes, and he offers no guarantees. For him, it is about helping citizens to act like citizens again.

His grassroots perspective of what it will take for the American people to help shape the future of their schools is both refreshing and hopeful. He knows that it won't happen in our legislative chambers, corporate boardrooms, or halls of academia. It can only happen where it began—where people gather and talk with one another.

A generation ago, the great American writer John Steinbeck drove an old pickup truck across our nation, accompanied only by a dog named Charley. He set out on his journey to see what had changed in this great country, but he was also looking for things that stayed the same. Somewhere along the way, he wrote that "there are still places where a pot of navy beans and fat-back can be had for dinner, and there are still times when friendship starts over a hot cup of coffee, laced with good conversation, between people of reason."

That sentiment may not hold much weight for those who see education in America as a set of goals to be met. But, for those who view education as a lifelong journey which brings together people in a way that defines community, it becomes a great place to start.

That is what Corky is about and why his unique perspective makes him eminently qualified to write this critically needed book.

Charles Irish
Former Superintendent of Schools
Medina City Schools, Medina, Ohio

Introduction

To the American People:

Think for a minute how we as a nation responded to the attack on Pearl Harbor, the leveling of the Twin Towers, the hurricane that plummeted the New Jersey coast, and the tornado that devastated Joplin, Missouri. We did what we always do when faced with a natural disaster or a threat to our national security. We came together, opened our wallets, rolled up our sleeves, and fixed the problem.

Stepping up to the plate and making a difference when we are needed is a deeply ingrained value in our culture, and it is not limited to big, life-changing events. In our communities, we are making a difference every day in less dramatic but important ways. Having worked with more than three hundred public school districts over the past twenty-five years, I have seen firsthand that we will nearly always respond to the educational needs of our children when we are asked to help and clearly see what is at stake—even when it means increasing our taxes.

Unfortunately, most of what we know about our schools is outdated and biased. It is based on a combination of our personal experience of having gone to school, the glowing reports of all the good things that are currently taking place in our local schools, and the overriding message coming from education reformers that our nation's public schools are failing and unable to compete in our global economy.

Today, most of us are in the dark about the extent to which the education reform movement in our country is impacting our local schools. We are unaware that our children are being over-tested, our teachers are physically exhausted and emotionally demoralized, and our tax dollars are being diverted by our elected representatives to replace our public schools with a privately managed, free-market system of education.

But what if we were able to clearly see what is happening? My purpose in writing this book is to let you, the American people, know how serious the current situation really is and what you can do about it.

Although it has been challenging at times, I have tried to be objective and avoid playing the blame game for who is at fault for what has happened. The truth of the matter is that we are all responsible for the current state of affairs. For the past century, we have been on a slow but steady track of delegating ownership of our schools to our education policymakers. As a result, America's schools are at a turning point.

In sharing early drafts of this book with a wide range of friends, colleagues, and acquaintances, many of them suggested that the book needed to include practical ways in which concerned citizens can get involved and make a difference. I heeded their valuable advice. In chapter 19, I include specific suggestions for what we can do as individual citizens to help shape the future of our nation's education system.

Thanks to the resiliency of the American spirit which is alive and well, I am confident that we can and will rise to the occasion as we always do when we know what is on the line and meet the urgent challenge now facing our public schools. Drawing upon the quote from John Lewis, a poor Alabama farmer in 1765, "If not us, who? If not now, when?"

Part I

How We Reached This Point

America's public schools did not reach what is now a pivotal turning point overnight. It has taken place gradually. For over a century, our government has been increasing the burden being placed upon our schools to meet the changing needs and expectations of our society.

Chapter 1

The Ever-Increasing Burden on America's Public Schools

Although Jamie Vollmer and I had met only briefly nearly twenty years ago, I felt compelled to call him after reading his new book. When he answered the phone, I explained that it was uncanny how similar our journeys into the world of the public schools had been and how closely our concerns about the impact of the education reform movement dovetailed.

Since our impromptu telephone conversation two years ago, we have stayed in touch with one another as we continue our personal journeys to give the American people a stronger voice in shaping the future of their schools. The first step in accomplishing this daunting but vitally important task is to fully understand the scope and magnitude of the ever-increasing burden currently being placed on America's public schools.

*   *   *

In 1988, the manager of a firm called the Great Midwestern Ice Cream Company was invited to serve on the Iowa Business and Education Roundtable. That manager, Jamie Vollmer, joined the roundtable to help make recommendations for improving Iowa's schools.

Back then, Jamie shared the view, common among his peers in the business community as well as among many of our political leaders, that our public schools were falling behind our international competitors, our way of life was at risk, and something needed to change. Like many others throughout our country, he blamed the problem on unionized teachers and overpaid school administrators who had no reason to change and no incentive to work hard.

To make a long story short, Jamie began to delve more deeply into what was actually taking place in the classrooms of our nation's schools and soon began to see a very different reality from the one that dominated—and, unfortunately, continues to dominate—the thinking of many of our business leaders and elected representatives. What he began to see was how the contract between our communities and our schools had changed. He saw how the role of our schools had transitioned from helping us teach our children to raising our kids.

In his book, *Schools Cannot Do It Alone*, Jamie includes a historical overview from the 1640s to the 2000s of how we as a society have increased what we are asking our public schools to do. With Jamie's permission, I am going to share his historical overview of the ever-increasing burden on America's public schools (Vollmer 2010, 32–35).

America's first schools appeared in the early 1640s and were designed to teach young people—originally white boys—basic reading, writing, and arithmetic while cultivating values that served our new democratic society. The founders of these schools assumed that families and churches bore the major responsibility for raising a child.

During the 1700s, some civics, history, science, and geography were introduced to the student's daily work, but the curriculum was limited and remained focused for 150 years. However, by the beginning of the twentieth century, America's leaders saw our public schools as the logical place to select and sort young people into two groups—thinkers and doers—according to the needs of the Industrial Age. It was at that time that we began to shift non-academic duties to the schools, and the trend has accelerated ever since.

From **1900 to 1910,** we shifted our public schools' responsibilities related to

- nutrition;
- immunization; and
- health (activities in the health arena multiply every year).

From **1910 to 1930,** we added

- physical education (including organized athletics);
- practical arts/domestic science/home economics (including sewing and cooking);
- vocational education (including industrial and agricultural education); and
- mandated school transportation.

In the **1940s,** we added

- business education (including typing, shorthand, and book-keeping);
- art and music;
- speech and drama;
- half-day kindergarten; and
- school lunch programs. (We take this for granted today, but it was a huge step to shift to the schools the job of feeding America's children one-third of their daily meals.)

In the **1950s,** we added

- expanded science and math education;
- safety education;

- driver's education;
- expanded music and art education;
- stronger foreign language requirements; and
- sex education. (Note that the topics continue to escalate.)

In the **1960s**, we added
- advanced placement programs;
- Head Start;
- Title 1;
- adult education;
- consumer education (resources, rights, and responsibilities);
- career education (options and entry-level skill requirements); and
- peace, leisure, and recreation education.

In the **1970s**, the breakup of the American family accelerated, and we added
- drug and alcohol abuse education;
- parenting education (techniques and tools for healthy parenting);
- behavior adjustment classes (including classroom and communication skills);
- character education;
- special education (mandated by the federal government);
- Title IX programs (greatly expanded athletic programs for girls);
- environmental education;
- African American heritage education; and
- school breakfast programs. (Now some schools feed America's children two-thirds of their daily meals throughout the school year and all summer. Sadly, these are the only decent meals some children receive.)

In the **1980s**, the floodgates opened and we added
- keyboarding and computer education;
- global education;
- multicultural/ethnic education;
- nonsexist education;
- English-as-a-second-language and bilingual education;
- teen pregnancy awareness;
- Hispanic heritage education;
- early childhood education;
- Jump Start, Early Start, Even Start, and Prime Start;
- full-day kindergarten;
- preschool programs for children at risk;
- after-school programs for children of working parents;
- alternative education in all forms;
- stranger danger education;
- antismoking education;
- sexual abuse prevention education;
- expanded health and psychological services; and
- child-abuse monitoring (a legal requirement for all teachers).

In the **1990s**, we added
- conflict resolution and peer mediation;
- HIV/AIDS education;
- CPR training;
- death education;
- America 2000 initiatives (Republican);
- inclusion;
- expanded computer and Internet education;
- distance learning;
- tech prep and school-to-work programs;
- technical adequacy assessment;
- postsecondary enrollment options;
- concurrent enrollment options;

- Goals 2000 initiatives (Democratic);
- expanded opportunities for talented and gifted students;
- at-risk and dropout prevention;
- homeless education (including causes and effects on children);
- gang education (in urban centers);
- service learning; and
- bus safety, bicycle safety, gun safety, and water safety education.

In the first decade of the twenty-first century, we have added
- No Child Left Behind (Republican);
- bully prevention;
- antiharassment policies (gender, race, religion, or national origin);
- elevator and escalator safety instruction;
- body mass index evaluation (obesity monitoring);
- organ donor education and awareness programs;
- personal financial literacy;
- entrepreneurial and innovation skills development;
- media literacy development;
- contextual learning skill development;
- health and wellness programs; and
- Race to the Top (Democratic).

It is important to note that this historical overview does not include the addition of multiple, specialized topics within each of the traditional subjects. It also does not include the explosion of standardized testing and test preparation activities or any of the onerous reporting requirements imposed by the federal government, such as four-year adjusted cohort graduation rates, parental notification of optional supplemental services, comprehensive restructuring plans, and reports of Adequate Yearly Progress. The impact of these and other mandates is discussed in the next chapter.

Once an outspoken critic, Jamie Vollmer has come full circle and is now one of our country's leading advocates for the importance of maintaining a healthy and viable system of public schools. Today, one of his major concerns—and mine as well—is that the ever-increasing burden being placed on our public schools has reached a critical point and needs to be addressed by the American people.

References

Vollmer, Jamie. 2010. *Schools Cannot Do It Alone: Building Public Support for America's Public Schools.* Fairfield, IA: Enlightenment Press.

Chapter 2

Accountability, School Choice, and High-Stakes Testing

Virtually every school superintendent and teacher I know believes he or she should be held accountable for meeting high educational standards. Many of them also support the idea of giving parents an opportunity to choose their children's school. However, as in many other things in life, too much of a good thing can become a big problem.

Today, our education policymakers are going too far, moving too quickly, and changing direction too often in their attempts to fix what, in their opinion, are our failing schools. In this chapter, I will discuss how the "ever-increasing burden on America's public schools" has become even more burdensome because of the growing obsession with accountability, school choice, and high-stakes testing by many education reformers.

In this and the next two chapters, I document how we have reached this critical point in our nation's history and then devote the final sections of the book to discussing the impact of what is happening and what the American people can do about it.

* * *

It all began in 1983 with the release of a report from the

National Commission on Excellence in Education called *A Nation at Risk: The Imperative for Educational Reform*. In the report, the commission wrote:

> Our Nation is at risk. Our once unchallenged preeminence in commerce, industry, science, and technological innovation is being overtaken by competitors throughout the world. This report is concerned with only one of the many causes and dimensions of the problem, but it is the one that undergirds American prosperity, security, and civility. We report to the American people that while we can take justifiable pride in what our schools and colleges have historically accomplished and contributed to the United States and the well-being of its people, the educational foundations of our society are presently being eroded by a rising tide of mediocrity that threatens our very future as a Nation and a people. What was unimaginable a generation ago has begun to occur—others are matching and surpassing our educational attainments. (National Commission on Excellence in Education 1983)

This dramatic report set into motion a domino effect of education reforms which are now affecting all of us. Today, our students are being over-tested, our teachers are overwhelmed and demoralized by the government mandates being placed on them, and our public education system is being replaced by a privately managed, free-market system of schooling. What's more, most Americans are in the dark about what is taking place.

At the outset, I want to make clear that I am not going to try to provide a detailed chronology of what has occurred since 1983. For that, I recommend that you read two books by Diane Ravitch who is regarded as an authority on the subject. The titles of her books are *The Death and Life of the Great American School System:*

How Testing and Choice Are Undermining Education and *Reign of Error: The Hoax of the Privatization Movement and the Danger to America's Public Schools.*

For the purpose of this book, I will report on four of the major education reform initiatives that have occurred since it was declared in *A Nation at Risk* that America's public schools are failing. These initiatives are Outcome-Based Education, the No Child Left Behind Act, Race to the Top, and the Common Core Standards.

Outcome-Based Education

In the early 1990s, following the urgent call to fix our "failing schools," a major education reform was introduced to our nation. It was called Outcome-Based Education.

Outcome-Based Education is grounded in the idea that academic success is best measured by what children actually learn as opposed to how long they are parked in their seats, how expansively multicultural their textbooks may be, or how much money is spent on their schooling. It is premised in real results, not pleasant intentions, and in assuring accountability in American education (Pearlstein 1994).

Early in its history, the Outcome-Based Education movement began encountering significant pushback. One of its major opponents was the Eagle Forum's Phyllis Schlafly who asserted that "in the name of school restructuring[,] OBE calls for a complete change in the way children are taught, graded[,] and graduated, kindergarten through twelfth grade. Since the American people seem ready to accept drastic surgery on our failed public schools, state departments of education are seizing this opportunity to force acceptance of OBE as the cure" (Schlafly 1993).

Phyllis Schlafly and others opposed to Outcome-Based Education contended that it was a process for government to tell our children how to live, what to say, what to think, what to know, and what not to know. Many opponents of Outcome-Based Education feared it would force children to conform to politically correct liberal ideology, attitudes, and behavior.

Although Outcome-Based Education eventually fell out of favor as the silver bullet to fix our public schools, the idea that academic success is best measured by what children actually learn survived the fallout of the political debate that took place. Since then, many states and school systems have adopted the philosophy by emphasizing outcomes that schools are expected to achieve. Few, however, have changed all of their rules and regulations to be compatible with the notion that every aspect of schooling must be based solely upon outcomes rather than upon other considerations such as length of the school year (Brandt 2014).

No Child Left Behind

In 2002, President George W. Bush signed into law a game-changing education reform initiative called No Child Left Behind. This law included strategies to increase accountability for states, school districts, and schools, provide greater choice for parents and students, give the states and local educational agencies more flexibility in the use of federal education dollars, and place a stronger emphasis on reading. It sounded pretty good at first.

However, the passage of No Child Left Behind changed the very nature of public schooling in our country by making standardized test scores the primary measure of school quality. The outcome of test scores in reading and mathematics became the new bar for judging students, teachers, principals, and schools. Testing and accountability were now our nation's education strategy.

Diane Ravitch was an early supporter of No Child Left Behind but changed her mind once she began to see the full impact of the law:

My support for NCLB remained strong until November 30, 2006. I can pinpoint the date exactly because that was the day I realized that NCLB was a failure. I went to a conference at the American Enterprise Institute—a well-respected conservative think tank—to hear a dozen or so scholars present their analyses of NCLB's remedies . . . The various presentations that day demonstrated that state education departments were drowning in new bureaucratic requirements, procedures, and routines, and that none of the prescribed remedies was making a difference (Ravitch 2010, 99).

She explained that, in her opinion, the most toxic flaw in NCLB was the legislative mandate that all students in every school must be proficient in reading and mathematics by 2014. The law included students with special needs and students whose native language is not English.

The two respected scholars who had organized the American Enterprise Institute conference referred to by Ravitch as well as other experts acknowledged that, while a worthy aspiration, the goal of 100 percent proficiency by 2014 was out of reach. Rather than being an incentive to improve teaching and learning, this unrealistic goal could destroy our education system by placing thousands of public schools at risk of being privatized, turned into charter schools, or closed.

Race to the Top

On February 17, 2009, President Obama signed into law legislation designed to stimulate the economy, support job creation, and invest in critical sectors, including education. The American Recovery and Reinvestment Act of 2009 authorized more than $50 billion in economic stimulus aid to prop up the budgets of our nation's public schools. One of the stipulations for receiving this money was that states had to publicly report data on dozens of key education indicators (McNeil 2014).

Under the American Recovery and Reinvestment Act, Congress also provided $4.35 billion for the Race to the Top Fund, a competitive grant program designed to encourage and reward states that are "creating the conditions for education innovation and reform; achieving significant improvement in student outcomes, including making substantial gains in student achievement, closing achievement gaps, improving high school graduation rates, and ensuring student preparation for success in college and careers; and implementing ambitious plans in four core education reform areas" (DOE 2009).

One of those core reform areas was building data systems that measure student growth and success and inform teachers and principals about how they can improve instruction. Secretary of Education Arne Duncan was particularly interested in applications in which "States propose working together to adapt one State's statewide longitudinal data system so that it may be used, in whole or in part, by one or more other States, rather than having each State build or continue building such systems independently" (DOE 2009).

To be eligible for the money, states also had to agree to adopt new Common Core Standards and tests, expand the number of charter schools, utilize student test scores to help evaluate the effectiveness of teachers, and agree to turn around their lowest-performing schools by firing staff, closing schools, and taking other dramatic steps.

While only eleven states and the District of Columbia won the Race to the Top funding, dozens of other states which had competed for the funds ended up accepting these education reform mandates as their new standards. With the new standards in place, the stage was set for what many believe is one of the biggest changes in education that has ever occurred in American history. That change is the adoption of the Common Core Standards.

Common Core Standards

Before discussing the far-reaching impact of the Common Core Standards, I would like to share a few observations. First of all, many school superintendents and teachers strongly support having more rigorous educational standards. They believe that, if effectively implemented, the Common Core Standards will significantly improve teaching and learning.

However, as the saying goes, the devil is in the details. While the goals of the Common Core Standards seem to make a lot of sense, the good intentions by education policymakers to "fix our schools" are already producing a number of negative, unintended consequences. One of these consequences is pushback by a growing number of parents and other concerned citizens against the Common Core Standards.

Much of this pushback, I believe, is based more upon how these standards were created and who created them than upon how effective they are educationally. For many people, their biggest concern is that they had no say in creating the standards and, as a result, they feel they are losing local control of their schools.

Finally, school superintendents and teachers are trapped in a major dilemma. On one hand, many of them strongly support the goals of the Common Core Standards and have invested a large amount of time, money, and emotional capital in a good-faith effort to comply with them. In fact, even in the early stages of implementing the new standards, many superintendents can point to significant progress in teaching and learning.

On the other hand, superintendents can see a number of pitfalls associated with the Common Core initiative—including a lack of time for teachers to adapt to the rigor of the new standards and the high-stakes tests that will be used to measure how students are doing. As a result, test scores will likely drop, teacher evaluations will be low, and school ratings will dip.

So, in a very real sense, the ironic twist being presented by the Common Core Standards is that by supporting them, our teachers and superintendents may be heading into a box canyon where they will be trapped and ambushed by education reformers who can point to the falling test scores and school ratings as further evidence that our current public schools are failing and need to be replaced with a free-market-driven educational system.

The truth of the matter is that the history of education reform is littered with the relics of initiatives that quickly enter the scene and then vanish when the political winds change direction and a new political party comes to power. So, it is anybody's guess how long the Common Core Standards will endure.

As a result of this political reality, the next chapter provides an in-depth look at the Common Core Standards initiative because it is current and includes valuable insight into the broad dynamics of the education reform movement in our country.

References

Brandt, Ron. June 2014. "An Overview of Outcome-Based Education." Lecture presented at the ASCD Conference on Teaching Excellence. Dallas, TX.

McNeil, Michele. May 6, 2014. "Stimulus Boosted State Data Systems, Despite Compliance Hurdles." Published online in *Education Week*.

National Commission of Excellence in Education. April 1983. *A Nation at Risk: The Imperative for Education Reform*.

Pearlstein, Mitchell. 1994. Foreword to "Outcome-Based Education: Has It Become More Affliction Than Cure?" by Bruno V. Manno, 3–4. Minneapolis: Center of the American Experiment.

Ravitch, Diane. 2010. *Life and Death of the Great American School System: How Testing and Choice Are Undermining Education.* New York: Basic Books.

Schlafly, Phyllis. May 1993. "What's Wrong With Outcome-Based Education?" *The Phyllis Schlafly Report.*

US Department of Education. 2009. "Race to the Top Program Executive Summary." Washington, DC: US Department of Education.

Chapter 3

An In-depth Look at the Common Core

In 2010, with the support and coordination of the National Governors Association Center and the Council of Chief State School Officers, the governors and state commissioners of education from forty-eight states, two territories, and the District of Columbia developed a common core of state standards in English language arts and mathematics for kindergarten through grade twelve. The effort was launched to ensure all students, regardless of where they live, graduate from high school prepared for college, career, and life. While the standards set grade-specific goals, they reportedly do not define how the standards should be taught or which materials should be used to support students (Common Core Standards Initiative 2014).

Currently, the vast majority of states have adopted and are implementing the Common Core Standards. In many of those states, the Common Core Standards will be much more rigorous than current state standards. As a result, student test scores and school ratings are expected to drop significantly—at least initially.

To my surprise

When I became aware of these new standards, I began asking school superintendents what they thought of them. To my surprise, instead of watching their eyes roll back in disgust and hearing the often-used phrase, "Here we go again—another government mandate," I heard something quite different.

What my superintendent colleagues told me is that they and many of their teachers strongly supported the goals of the Common Core Standards. They supported the goal of challenging students to think more critically and more effectively solve problems. They supported the goal of increasing the rigor of their state tests and to stop lowering the thresholds of what it takes to pass these tests so more students could meet minimum educational standards.

Prior to the introduction of the Common Core Standards, some public schools had already been moving in the direction of teaching higher-level thinking skills. As Bob Scott, superintendent of the Avon Lake City Schools in Avon Lake, Ohio, explained, "Although we were on our way to meeting the goals of the Common Core, adoption of these new state standards helped bring all of our staff members together and double their efforts to help our students to think more creatively."

He added that, in meeting this important goal, teachers must be able to maintain a balanced learning environment and not just teach to the high-stakes test that will be used to measure how well students are doing in meeting the new educational standards. He believes that one of the major challenges facing his teachers is withstanding the pressure on them to teach to the test because they will be personally evaluated based upon the test results of their students.

Local community values

A growing number of superintendents believe that while our nation should have rigorous educational standards that are common for all students, it is important to balance this larger educational framework with the local needs of our schools and communities. To put some weight behind these words, the Board of Education in a small, rural school district in western Ohio passed a resolution reaffirming its commitment to its citizens to balance its district's implementation of the Common Core State Standards with the local values of its community.

In the preamble to its resolution, the Fort Recovery Board of Education stated that, while continuing to follow Ohio's Common Core Standards, it will remain responsible locally for developing the curriculum, lesson plans, textbooks, and other instructional materials which reflect the values of the local community. The Board said it will "fight vigorously to defend and maintain that local control" and that it will "remain vigilant in safeguarding the instruction of our children."

Timelines and testing

In addition to their concern about aligning the Common Core Standards with local community values, many superintendents and teachers are deeply concerned about the implementation timelines and the testing which they view as being unrealistic and unfair. They know it will take more time than is currently being given to them to align their school districts' teaching strategies and curricula with the new standards and feel it is unfair to judge how well their students are doing after only two years of implementation. Many superintendents believe our teachers will need at least five years to fully adapt what they are doing in the classroom to these highly rigorous educational standards.

With regard to the high-stakes tests being created to measure student performance against the Common Core Standards, as of the writing of this book, the situation appears to be fluid. For example, one of the high-stakes tests, Partnership for Assessment of Readiness for College and Career (PARCC), being used in several states, is not ready, according to many superintendents.

They have several concerns about the PARCC tests. One is that the tests do not provide data that will provide insight into the educational needs of students. Second, the tests take decision making and control of the curriculum away from the teachers and administrators who best know the needs of our students. Third, data from the PARCC tests will be used to provide a state rating for schools and teachers and does not account for the many important intangible qualities and skills that our talented educators possess. And, fourth, the cost of implementing these tests will be forced on the residents of local school districts which have no choice in the matter.

One superintendent from a school district near Cincinnati, Ohio, stated what many others are thinking: "I'm worried that we will get mowed over by the PARCC assessments. I'm concerned that not enough time is being taken to effectively develop these high-stakes tests and that the low test scores of our students will then be used against us. I fear that anyone who wants to throw our public schools under the bus will use these low test scores to justify imposing more government control over what we do. We need to take a two- or three-year sabbatical from PARCC, involve our local educators, parents, and community leaders in what we are doing, and then do it correctly. Right now, we are trying to build the proverbial plane while it is in the air."

When another superintendent from a school district in northeast Ohio shared examples of the Common Core test questions on mathematics with several engineers attending a Rotary Club luncheon, he said they had a difficult time even understanding the questions—let alone coming up with the answers. He added that they approached him after the luncheon and asked what they could do to help deal with the situation.

As with previous reform initiatives, the Common Core Standards place the responsibility for improving education solely upon our schools. Our schools, however, have a limited amount of influence over a child's education. Between the time a child enters school and graduates, he or she only spends 14 percent of his or her time there (Bransford, Brown, and Cocking 1999, Fig. 1.2).

Since the vast majority of a student's life is spent outside the classroom, parents and the community share a significant portion of the responsibility for educating that student. This includes helping to assure that the Common Core Standards are closely aligned with local family and community values.

National confirmation

In an opinion survey conducted in 2014 by the American Association of School Administrators, our nation's superintendents confirmed what I have been reporting in this chapter. While most of them are convinced that the Common Core Standards will significantly improve teaching and learning, many are concerned about the implementation timelines and testing.

The AASA report (Finnan 2014) shows that most of the superintendents surveyed have already begun to implement the new standards and that 92.5 percent of them think the Common Core Standards are much more rigorous than previous standards. In addition, superintendents believe that the new standards will increase students' critical thinking skills and ensure they are better prepared for college and the modern workforce.

Similar to what I am hearing from my friends and colleagues, superintendents in the nationwide AASA study are concerned about the high-stakes testing that is tied to the Common Core Standards. Many of them believe that delaying the testing would give them more of an opportunity to implement the standards and prepare their schools for the tests. They think that a delay in implementing these tests would also improve community and teacher support for the standards.

For one veteran superintendent from a school district west of Phoenix, Arizona, the concern is not about the new standards themselves. Rather, it is about the possibility that they could be discarded if political pressure to get rid of them becomes too great. This, she said, would be a disaster. It would be like throwing the baby out with the bathwater because she is already finding that the new standards are making a positive difference for her students. Her advice is to protect and preserve the goals of the Common Core and turn over control of how these goals are implemented to our local schools.

Growing resistance

Many superintendents share her concern about the growing pressure to get rid of these new educational standards—and for good reason. For a number of groups and organizations, the term *Common Core* has become a symbol of government overreach and loss of local control of our schools. One of those groups is Ohioans Against Common Core, which has prominently displayed on the homepage of its website the group's stated goal of affirming parental control, restoring local control, and reducing the power of standardized testing (Ohioans Against Common Core 2014).

The desire of citizens to take back local control of their schools is also why Indiana Governor Mike Pence said he signed a bill on March 24, 2014, making Indiana the first state to withdraw from the Common Core math and reading standards. In signing the bill, he said he believes students are best served by education decisions made at the state and local level.

> I believe when we reach the end of this process there are going to be many other states around the country that will take a hard look at the way Indiana has taken a step back, designed our own standards and done it in a way where we drew on educators, we drew on citizens, we drew on parents and developed standards that meet the needs of our people (Ballentine and LoBianco 2014).

While Indiana is the first state to take an official stand, resistance to the Common Core Standards initiative is growing throughout the country. More than two hundred bills on the national standards were introduced in 2014 and about half would slow or halt their implementation, according to the National Conference of State Legislatures. That is about an 85 percent increase from 2013.

To address the growing public pressure to abandon the Common Core Standards, some states are playing the rebranding game. While they are keeping the new standards, they are getting rid of the name, *Common Core*, and replacing it with a name that is more politically acceptable. In Iowa, for example, *Common Core* is called *Iowa Core*. In Arizona, the Common Core name was scrubbed from the state's math and reading standards. And, in Florida, the Common Core name has been changed to the *Next Generation Sunshine State Standards*.

Even though many of the major teacher unions have strongly supported the Common Core Standards from their inception and most teachers embrace the goal of teaching higher-level thinking skills, some are beginning to back away from the new educational standards (*Arizona Daily Star* 2014, A9). The heads of the two national teacher unions, the National Education Association and American Federation of Teachers, say they support the standards but contend that implementation has been so rushed and so botched that adjustments, and even delay, are in order.

In addition, the Chicago Teachers Union which represents teachers in the third largest school district in our country and the New York State Teachers United have withdrawn their support for the Common Core Standards. While not coming out and opposing the Common Core Standards, teacher associations in a number of states have been instrumental in getting lawmakers to approve a delay in administering the high-stakes tests that students must take to meet the standards.

From a national perspective, Diane Ravitch, who once served as assistant secretary in charge of the Office of Educational Research and Improvement in the US Department of Education, says she has long advocated for voluntary national standards. She has indicated, however, that at least for now she cannot support the Common Core Standards. Her blog shares some of her concerns and raises important questions that put into clear perspective much of what is taking place in the education reform arena:

> For the past two years, I have steadfastly insisted that I was neither for nor against the Common Core standards. I was agnostic. I wanted to see how they worked in practice. I wanted to know, based on evidence, whether or not they improve education and whether they reduce or increase the achievement gaps among different racial and ethnic groups.
>
> After much deliberation, I have come to the conclusion that I can't wait five or ten years to find out whether test scores go up or down, whether or not schools improve, and whether the kids now far behind are worse off than they are today.
>
> I have come to the conclusion that the Common Core standards effort is fundamentally flawed by the process with which they have been foisted upon the nation.
>
> The Common Core standards have been adopted in 46 states and the District of Columbia without any field test. They are being imposed on the children of this nation despite the fact that no one has any idea how they will affect students, teachers, or schools. We are a nation of guinea pigs, almost all trying an unknown new program at the same time.
>
> Maybe the standards will be great. Maybe they will be a disaster. Maybe they will improve achievement. Maybe they will widen the achievement gaps between haves and have-nots. Maybe they will cause the children who now struggle to give up altogether. Would the Federal Drug Administration approve the use of a drug with no trials, no concern for possible harm or unintended consequences?

President Obama and Secretary Duncan often say that the Common Core standards were developed by the states and voluntarily adopted by them. This is not true. They were developed by an organization called Achieve and the National Governors Association, both of which were generously funded by the Gates Foundation. There was minimal public engagement in the development of the Common Core. Their creation was neither grassroots nor did it emanate from the states.

In fact, it was well understood by states that they would not be eligible for Race to the Top funding ($4.35 billion) unless they adopted the Common Core standards. Federal law prohibits the U.S. Department of Education from prescribing any curriculum, but in this case the Department figured out a clever way to evade the letter of the law. Forty-six states and the District of Columbia signed on, not because the Common Core standards were better than their own, but because they wanted a share of the federal cash. In some cases, the Common Core standards really were better than the state standards, but in Massachusetts, for example, the state standards were superior and well tested but were ditched anyway and replaced with the Common Core. The former Texas State Commissioner of Education, Robert Scott, has stated for the record that he was urged to adopt the Common Core standards before they were written.

She continues:

Another reason I cannot support the Common Core standards is that I am worried that they will cause a precipitous decline in test scores, based on arbitrary cut scores, and this will have a disparate impact on students who are

English language learners, students with disabilities, and students who are poor and low-performing. A principal in the Midwest told me that his school piloted the Common Core assessments and the failure rate rocketed upwards, especially among the students with the highest needs. He said the exams looked like AP exams and were beyond the reach of many students.

When Kentucky piloted the Common Core, proficiency rates dropped by 30 percent. The Chancellor of the New York Board of Regents has already warned that the state should expect a sharp drop in test scores.

What is the purpose of raising the bar so high that many more students fail (Ravitch 2013)?

One final concern

As I reported in the previous chapter, one of the stipulations for receiving more than $50 billion from the American Recovery and Reinvestment Act of 2009 was that states had to publicly report data on dozens of key education indicators which were subsequently embedded in the Race to the Top initiative and Common Core Standards. With public trust and confidence in our federal government at all-time lows, there is growing concern about providing our government officials with this amount of personal information about our students and their families.

The American Principles Project is one group expressing its concern about this student tracking database. A conservative education think tank, it reported in 2011 that the Common Core's technological project is one part of a much broader plan by the federal government to track individuals from birth through their participation in the workforce.

The American Principles Project charged that these systems will aggregate massive amounts of personal data—including health-care histories, income information, religious affiliations, voting status, and even blood types and homework completion. The data will then be available to a wide variety of public agencies, despite federal student-privacy protections guaranteed by the Family Educational Rights and Privacy Act, and will pave the way for private entities to buy their way into this personal data collection system (Malkin 2013).

The challenge

As I conclude this chapter, the fate of the Common Core Standards is yet to be determined. Although many, if not most, teachers and superintendents embrace the primary goal of these standards—which is to provide our students with higher-level thinking skills—the Common Core Standards initiative is posing two major problems that need to be addressed.

The first problem involves the high-stakes testing being developed to measure how students are progressing based upon the new standards. Superintendents who have seen these tests report, thus far, that they are confusing and unfair, and since the tests will be used to help evaluate teacher performance and generate school ratings, they should be shelved until they are improved.

The second problem plaguing the Common Core Standards is the growing pushback against them from citizens who view them as another government mandate and an attempt to take away local control. Some educators predict they will eventually disappear and join the list of other education reform initiatives that have lost their luster and are no longer in vogue.

To prevent the goals of the Common Core Standards from being discarded due to real and imagined implementation problems and concerns, I have three specific suggestions:

1. Since we tend not to trust what we cannot see, superintendents need to remove the cloak of darkness surrounding the Common Core Standards. They need to sit down with the

citizens of their communities and openly discuss all aspects of these standards—including the good, the bad, and the ugly.

2. The American people need to be assured that, with their help, our children are not going to be over-tested, the testing is going to be rigorous but fair, and what is taught is going to reflect local values and aspirations. To accomplish this goal, school officials, parents, and other community members need to work closely together in carefully monitoring the selection of textbooks and other educational materials.

3. The American people need to provide our teachers with the time and staff development they need to effectively teach to the new standards. Many, if not most, of our teaching staffs are overwhelmed by the implementation deadlines and other unrealistic expectations now being placed on them.

While the future of the Common Core Standards may be uncertain, one thing is crystal clear. Despite the fact that school superintendents and teachers had little or no input into the creation of these standards and the American people were left out of the process altogether, early indications show that these new standards are having both a positive and negative impact.

In section II of this book, I discuss how the education reform movement and the Common Core Standards are impacting our children, our teachers, and our communities. But, first, I want to focus on the integrity of the data being used to reform our nation's education system.

References

Ballentine, Summer, and Tom LoBianco. 2014, March 24. "Indiana Withdrawing from Common Core Standards." Associated Press.

Bransford, John D., Brown, Ann L. and Rodney R. Cocking. 1999. *How People Learn: Brain, Mind, Experience, and School.* Washington, DC: National Academy Press.

Common Core State Standards Initiative. 2014, September 9. http://www.corestandards.org/about-the-standards/.

Finnan, Leslie. 2014. "Common Core and Other State Standards: Superintendents Feel Optimism, Concern and Lack of Support." Alexandria, VA: The School Superintendents' Association.

Malkin, Michelle. 2013, March 8. "Rotten to the Core: The Fed's Invasive Student Tracking Database." Creators Syndicate.

Ohioans Against Common Core: Affirming Parental Control, Restoring Local Control, Reducing Power of Standardized Testing. 2014, September 9. http://ohioansagainstcommoncore.com/.

Ravitch, Diane. 2013, February 26. "Why I Cannot Support the Common Core Standards." http://dianeravitch.net/2013/02/26/why-i-cannot-support-the-common-core-standards/.

Arizona Daily Star. 2014, May 14. Page A9. Editorial page writers. "Teacher Unions Out to Sabotage Common Core."

Chapter 4

How Our Schools Are Really Doing

At the time I began writing this chapter, our states had spent hundreds of millions of dollars on testing and on test preparation materials. Some states were testing children in the early grades and in prekindergarten in order to prepare them for testing that began in the third grade, and some schools were allocating up to 20 percent of the school year to preparing for state tests.

In Texas, school reformers had mandated that students needed to pass fifteen different tests to earn a high school diploma (Ravitch 2013, 13, 247). I will discuss in chapter 18 how that state mandate has been reduced from fifteen to five as a result of resistance from parents and other citizens who now recognize what is happening to their public schools.

Before sharing what the research says about how our nation's public schools are really doing, I would like to begin by highlighting a great irony that is now taking place. While leaders of the education reform movement in our country are trying to model our education system after countries whose students have historically outperformed America's students on high-stakes tests, some of those very same countries are trying to make their education system more like ours.

Take, for example, China.

A Great Irony

Dr. Yong Zhao is an internationally known scholar who studies the impact of globalization and technology on education. He is also author of the book *Who's Afraid of the Big Bad Dragon: Why China Has the World's Best and Worst Education.*

Dr. Zhao explains that China has an effective system to prepare students to pass exams. It is a system that includes devoted parents and diligent students who are convinced that the only path to a worthy life is passing the exam and who are punished or rewarded according to their exam results. However, unless the Chinese only want obedient, compliant, and homogeneous workers, they know they have to shift the emphasis of their educational system.

The West, according to Dr. Zhao, is where China is working to find the inspiration it desperately needs for this new educational focus because, as the Chinese Ministry of Education pointed out a decade ago, its exam-oriented education system does not work for the new world:

> The exams-oriented education refers to the factual existence in our nation's education of the tendency to simply prepare for tests, aim for high test scores, and blindly pursue admission rates (to colleges or higher-level schools) while ignoring the real needs of the student and societal development. It pays attention to only a minority of the student population and neglects the majority; it emphasizes knowledge transmission but neglects moral, physical, aesthetic and labor education, as well as the cultivation of applied abilities and psychological and emotional development; it relies on rote memorization and mechanical drills as the primary approach, which makes learning uninteresting, hinders students from learning actively, prevents them from taking initiatives and heavily burdens them with

excessive amounts of course work; it uses test scores as the primary or only criterion to evaluate students, hurting their motivation and enthusiasm, squelching their creativity and impeding their overall development (Zhao 2014).

According to Michael Fullan and Andy Hargreaves who also have studied effective educational systems in other countries, they don't do what we are doing in the United States. Unlike us, Finland, Singapore, Canada, and other successful countries don't reward or punish teachers with measures like test-driven, performance-based pay and other strategies which are leading to teacher burnout and causing veteran teachers to leave their profession. Instead, they develop the entire teaching profession to the point where students encounter good teachers one after another (Fullan and Hargreaves 2012).

The fact that our education policymakers are trying to pattern America's education system after China or other countries whose students perform well on high-stakes tests while they are trying to emulate us raises an important question: How are our schools really doing?

In *50 Myths & Lies That Threaten America's Public Schools: The Real Crisis in Education*, the authors challenge many of the assumptions about the quality of education being provided by our nation's public schools. In discussing why they wrote their book, they explain:

Why we have written this book should be obvious. The education of America's children is one of its most important priorities. That message has been lost on many Americans. We cannot count the number of even our close acquaintances who recite warped opinions about our nation's public schools: They are inferior to private schools; they are among the worst in the world in math and science; teachers should be fired if students don't score at the national average, and on and on. Many citizens' conception of K–12 public education in the United States is more myth than reality. It is essential that the truth replace the fiction (Berliner and Glass 2014, 3).

These myths are largely responsible for the obsession that many of our education reformers have with accountability, school choice, and high-stakes testing. Unfortunately, these myths have rarely been challenged and almost never discussed by the American people.

For the remainder of this chapter, I am going to challenge a number of major myths about our public schools and shed some light on how our schools are really doing.

* * *

The myth: International test scores show that the United States has a second-rate education system.

The facts: International test scores are poor indicators to use in ranking the quality of national education systems and are even worse in predicting future national prosperity. The United States, recognizably the most prosperous nation on the planet, has never fared well on international test comparisons of student achievement in math or science. In 1964, we took eleventh place among twelve countries participating in the first major international study of student achievement in math. One of the major reasons why we rank so low on international test scores is that our child poverty rate exceeds 20 percent—which is considerably higher than comparable countries. In Finland, for example, the child poverty rate is less than 5 percent. If we looked only at the students in the United States who attend schools where child poverty rates are under 10 percent, we would rank as the number one country in the world on international tests (Berliner and Glass 2014, 12–17).

*   *   *

The myth: Charter schools are better than traditional public schools.

The facts: The first national assessment of charter schools was reported by the Center for Research on Educational Outcomes at Stanford University in 2009. The study found that more than 80 percent of charter schools are either no better or are worse than traditional public schools at securing gains in math and reading for their students. The CREDO report released in 2013 updates the 2009 data and reveals that traditional public schools outperform charter schools in math and reading (Berliner and Glass 2014, 22–26).

*   *   *

The myth: Cyberschools are an efficient, cost-saving, and highly effective means of delivering education.

The facts: Online charter schools, also known as cyberschools, enroll students in full-time schooling delivered over the Internet and have become a fast-growing alternative to traditional brick-and-mortar public education. The National Education Policy Center estimated in 2013 that 300 full-time cyberschools enrolled more than 200,000 students throughout the United States. When the performance of children who receive their education at cyberschools is assessed, the results, however, are dismal. Dropout rates for cyberschooled students often exceed 50 percent; the graduation rate for these students is about two-thirds the rate for traditional schools and student-teacher ratios are as high as 200 to 1 in some cyberschools. When it comes to student achievement, children educated in cyberschools lag far behind children educated in traditional brick-and-mortar public schools. State department of education ratings of cyberschools in 2011–12 showed that more than 70 percent were rated as academically unacceptable (Berliner and Glass 2014, 31–35).

* * *

The myth: School choice and competition work to improve all schools.

The facts: Many education reformers believe that vouchers, tuition tax credits, and charter schools inject competition into the education system and "raise all boats." The facts, however, say something quite different. The real impact of school choice and competition is that students who leave their public school to attend a charter school are often the ones with the most resources. They have better academic skills and higher motivation, they have more involved and better-educated parents, and they have access to personal transportation so they can get to and from schools that are not in their neighborhood. As a result, rather than raising all boats by offering all students better educational opportunities, vouchers and charter schools often use tax dollars to help some students while leaving many others even more segregated and disadvantaged (Berliner and Glass 2014, 41–45).

* * *

The myth: Teachers should be evaluated on the basis of the performance of their students.

The facts: Merit pay is one of the strategies being utilized by a number of states to evaluate and motivate their teachers. The premise of merit pay is that teachers will be paid more money than their colleagues if their students perform better on high-stakes tests. The fallacy of this premise is that most teachers are not motivated primarily by money. In addition to the fact that what teachers do is hard to measure accurately, merit pay systems can promote corruption and impede teacher collaboration. Cheating on reporting test scores already has occurred in Atlanta, Washington, DC, and a dozen other cities. To accurately identify the educational needs of today's students, teachers must work together. However, since merit pay systems are often based upon the performance of their students, teachers are incentivized to attract the most affluent students to their classrooms and focus more upon their success and less on the success of students in other teachers' classrooms (Berliner and Glass 2014, 58–63).

*   *   *

The myth: Class size does not matter.

The facts: A few years ago, I learned firsthand the importance of class size while working with a group of educational leaders who were trying to figure out what to do about an overcrowding problem in their schools. To better understand the scope of the problem, we asked their building principals to invite one or two of their most effective teachers to a meeting to discuss the situation. I remember, as if it were yesterday, the response to my question, "How important is class size?" One of the teachers looked at me as if I had lost my mind and said, "You've got to be kidding me. Class size is extremely important. I've had classes with thirty students and classes with twenty students. With large classes, I am simply unable to reach a half dozen or more of my students." In addition to this personal anecdote, one of the most credible studies on class size occurred in Tennessee in 1985. Project Star showed that smaller class size—classes with fewer than eighteen students—had a significant impact for students in grades K–3. These students scored better on standardized tests, earned better grades in their classes, and exhibited continued improvement beyond the early grades. Today's classroom is dramatically different from what it was like when I went to school. Instead of sitting in rows, copying information from the blackboard, and then repeating that information on a multiple choice test, education is now much more individualized. With smaller classes, teachers can spend more time with each of their students (Berliner and Glass 2014, 89–92).

*   *   *

The myth: Money does not matter.

The facts: Many critics of our public schools believe the taxpayers are pouring large sums of money down the drain of a broken education system. They argue that while the cost of running our schools is increasing, we have little to show for it when we look at test scores. Their conclusion is that money doesn't matter. However, the claim that the cost of running our public schools has been skyrocketing while student achievement has remained flat is refuted by the facts. According to long-term trend data from the National Assessment of Educational Progress, all subgroups of American students are showing substantial improvement. Decades of research have concluded that money really does matter in education. Studies, for example, consistently show that more experienced teachers—who receive higher salaries—are more effective than lower-salaried teachers with less experience. Studies also show that consistently higher salaries attract better candidates to the teaching profession, help keep them in the profession, and reduce teacher turnover rates in high-poverty schools. Today, our public schools are expected and required to meet the needs of every student who shows up at the schoolhouse door. As a result, providing thirteen years of quality education for all of our students costs a lot of money (Berliner and Glass 2014, 171–175).

*   *   *

The myth: Our nation is suffering because our educational system is not producing enough scientists, engineers, and mathematicians.

The facts: This myth began in the 1950s when Sputnik launched the space race between the United States and the Soviet Union. In 2008, the National Science Board reported that more than seventeen million students had earned college degrees in science, technology, engineering, and math. At the same time, fewer than seven million jobs were available to them. In 2004, despite concerns about shortages of science, technology, engineering, and math personnel in the US workforce, there was no evidence of any shortages since at least 1990, and none were projected in the future. The research also indicates that a growing number of US students are studying math and science. Since 1990, the percentage of students earning calculus credits in high school has more than doubled and the percentage of students earning physics, chemistry, and advanced biology credits has increased more than 50 percent. Over the past twenty to thirty years, the scores on math tests and most science tests have been gradually improving for America's students. In 2006, for example, a report from the Program for International Student Assessment showed that 7.4 million American students scored in the top two categories of performance in science (Berliner and Glass 2014, 203–213).

* * *

The myth: Education will lift the poor out of poverty and materially enrich our entire nation.

The facts: In the nineteenth century, Horace Mann, commonly known as the father of our current system of public schools, believed that public education would eliminate poverty by increasing intelligence. Today, 20 percent of America's children live in poverty and our policymakers are still trying to address the poverty problem through education. While education can benefit both individuals and our economy in many ways, the evidence shows that education cannot by itself end poverty. There are a number of reasons why this is true. First of all, education's influence is too indirect to address today's poverty. Education is about what will happen for the next generation rather than the current generation. Second, although there is evidence that some schools with many low-income students are academically successful, there is much more evidence that most schools do not overcome poor health, housing instability, and other barriers that stem from poverty. Third, while educational attainment is correlated with higher income, the financial benefit is lower for women, people of color, and children of parents with lower-than-average socioeconomic status. For instance, in 2008 the annual median income for Asian males with a bachelor's degree was $63,300 while the annual median income for Hispanic females with the identical level of education was only $41,000. Fourth, our nation's unemployment rate is not going to be substantially reduced because of education. For example, between 2007 and 2009 when the unemployment rate more than doubled, there was relatively no change in the quality or quantity of education in our nation. Finally, a well-educated America does not guarantee economic prosperity. Today, hundreds of thousands of people with advanced degrees in law, engineering, and other professions are unable to find work in their chosen fields (Berliner and Glass 2014, 228–233).

*   *   *

The myth: The schools are wasting their time trying to teach problem solving, creativity, and other higher-level thinking skills.

The facts: Students are equipped with the ability to solve problems and think creatively long before they start going to school. From a very early age, children find many ways to demonstrate both creativity and problem solving. The research clearly shows that by tapping into this natural childhood instinct and the wealth of knowledge that children bring to school, teachers are able to engage their students in meaningful classroom conversation and dialogue which teaches them creativity, problem solving and other high-order thinking skills. And they can accomplish it while also providing students with important information that they need to memorize and know (Berliner and Glass 2014, 238–241).

One of my goals in writing this book is to paint an accurate picture of how our schools are really doing. To accomplish this task, I have drawn upon both my grassroots experience of working with local schools and communities and the work of respected professionals who conduct high-quality educational research.

The facts generated by the extensive research of David Berliner and Gene Glass serve as an important reality check on the validity of the myths that are driving education reform in our nation. In reflecting upon these facts, I have some thoughts that I would like to share.

First, the intellectual foundation of our country's education reform movement has, at the very least, significant cracks in it. As the facts presented above clearly show, the assumptions used to justify our nation's current education reforms are now being challenged and need to be discussed by the American people.

Second, if even just a portion of the challenges to these myths is true, our public schools are in more trouble than we may think because the education reform movement draws its energy from them. As a result, little will change until the American people recognize what is happening to our schools and get involved in helping shape their future.

Finally, what matters even more than how much of this information may or may not be true is the fact that the American people did not have an opportunity to discuss the education reform measures currently impacting our schools before they were mandated into law. In fact, with a few rare exceptions, our local superintendents and teachers had very little, if anything, to say about the major thrust of these reforms.

The harsh reality is that influential voices in the US Department of Education, in the big foundations, on Wall Street, and in the major corporations now agree upon how to reform American education. In the next chapter, I identify who they are and what scope their influence has.

References

Berliner, David C. and Gene V. Glass. 2014. *50 Myths & Lies That Threaten America's Public Schools: The Real Crisis in Education.* New York: Columbia University Teachers College Press.

Fullan, Michael, and Andy Hargreaves. 2012, June 6. "Reviving Teaching with Professional Capital." *Education Week.*

Ravitch, Diane. 2013. *Reign of Error: The Hoax of the Privatization Movement and the Danger to America's Public Schools.* New York: Alfred A. Knopf.

Zhao, Yong. 2014, February 22. "Déjà vu: Too Late to Learn from China." http://zhaolearning.com/2014/02/22/deja-vu-too-late-to-learn-from-china/.

Chapter 5

The Corporate Takeover of Our Schools

Throughout my career, I have spent a significant amount of time working with our elected officials at all levels of government. As a result, I think that I am fairly savvy about how our political system operates. Yet, after conducting the research for this book, I was surprised to learn how much the ultimate fate of our education system rests in the hands of just a relative handful of rich and powerful people.

What I have concluded from my research is that, while our elected representatives may be passing the laws designed to improve our public schools, they are only the tip of the iceberg when it comes to who is influencing education reform in our country. Beneath the surface supporting them is a close-knit network of powerful think-tank research organizations representing our major political parties and all philosophical points of view—liberal, centrist, right, and far right.

However, if you want to know who is really driving education reform and determining the fate of our public schools, all you need to do is unpeel one more layer of the education reform onion and follow the money.

Follow the money

As most people know, Bill Gates is one of the richest and most philanthropic individuals in the world. But what most people may not know is that he has his fingers on the pulse of most of the key players in the education reform movement.

Just for starters, in addition to underwriting the expansion of charter schools, test-based evaluation of teachers, and merit pay for teachers, the Bill and Melinda Gates Foundation has made grants to the American Federation of Teachers and the National Education Association and subsidizes many of the major think tanks in Washington, DC. His foundation has also been a major financial supporter of the Common Core Standards.

For example, *Education Week* reported that the Bill and Melinda Gates Foundation had increased funding for education advocacy groups from $276,000 in 2002 to nearly $57 million in 2005 (Ravitch, 2010, 210). These groups included Achieve, the architect of the Common Core Standards ($8.84 million), Alliance for Excellent Education ($3 million), Center on Education Policy ($963,000), Council of Chief State School Officers, also a key player in the creation and support of the Common Core Standards ($25.48 million), Education Sector ($290,000), Education Trust ($5.8 million), National Alliance for Public Charter Schools ($800,000), National Association for Secondary School Principals ($2.1 million), National Association of State Boards of Education ($224,000), National Conference of State Legislatures ($682,000), National Governors Association, another key supporter of the Common Core Standards initiative ($21.23 million), Progressive Policy Institute ($510,000), and Thomas B. Fordham Institute ($848,000).

In addition to the Bill and Melinda Gates Foundation, two other major funders of school reform are having a significant influence on education policy in our country. They are the Eli and

Edythe Broad Foundation and the Walton Family Foundation (Ravitch 2010, 200).

The Eli and Edythe Broad Foundation has invested millions of dollars in charter schools, pay-for-performance programs for teachers, programs that bypass traditional routes into teaching and school leadership, and a wide range of education advocacy groups. These groups include the Center for American Progress, California Charter School Association, Center for Education Reform, Council for the Great City Schools, Council of Chief State School Officers, National Governors Association, Thomas B. Fordham Institute, American Enterprise Institute, Black Alliance for Education Options, Education Sector, and Education Trust (Ravitch 2010, 216).

A third major funder of education reform is the Walton Family Foundation. Established by Sam Walton, the founder of Walmart, the Walton Family Foundation has been the strongest and most consistent funder in the nation advancing school choice (Ravitch 2010, 202). In 2007, for example, the Foundation awarded $82 million to charter schools, $26 million to school choice programs, and $8 million to school reform activities in Arkansas and Mississippi.

In 2007, the Walton Family Foundation also made significant contributions to organizations advocating for vouchers. These organizations included the Alliance for School Choice ($1.6 million), Children's Educational Opportunity Foundation ($4 million), Hispanic Council for Reform and Educational Options ($700,000), and Black Alliance for Educational Options ($850,000) (Ravitch 2010, 202).

Clearly, education reform in our country is not a grassroots movement. Superintendents and teachers have had very little, if any, input into the reforms that are driving education in our schools while the American people have had none. Instead, the school reform movement is being driven by education advocacy groups that receive significant amounts of funding from a relatively small group of wealthy philanthropists with specific agendas.

Diane Ravitch shares her concern about this concentration of corporate power:

> These foundations, no matter how worthy and high-minded, are after all, not public agencies. They are not subject to public oversight or review, as a public agency would be. They have taken it upon themselves to reform public education, perhaps in ways that would never survive the scrutiny of voters in any district or state. If voters don't like the foundations' reform agenda, they can't vote them out of office. The foundations demand that public schools and teachers be held accountable for performance, but they themselves are accountable to no one. If their plans fail, no sanctions are levied against them. They are bastions of unaccountable power (Ravitch 2010, 200–201).

The corporate takeover of our schools, however, extends beyond the powerful influence of the Gates, Broad, and Walton foundations. It also includes Wall Street hedge fund managers and firms that manage charter schools.

Wall Street hedge fund managers

Wall Street hedge fund managers became interested in the charter school movement for a couple of reasons. First, they believed charter schools would benefit poor children. Secondly, the billions of dollars pumped into the public schools each year provided them an opportunity to make money on real estate and educational services (Ravitch 2013, 160–161).

To influence education policy, they support the political campaigns of individuals who support their agenda. One of the groups they support is Democrats for Education Reform which raises money for candidates and elected officials who advocate for the expansion of charter schools and the imposition of teacher evaluation systems based on test scores (Ravitch 2013, 26).

In addition to contributing to political campaigns, hedge fund managers work hand-in-hand with political and corporate allies that support the charter school movement. Lee Fang of *The Nation* describes one of their conferences:

> Standing at the lectern of Arizona State University's SkySong conference center in April (2011), investment banker Michael Moe exuded confidence as he kicked off his second annual conference of education startup companies and venture capitalists. A press packet cited reports that rapid changes in education could unlock immense potential for entrepreneurs. "This education issue," Moe declared, "there's not a bigger problem or bigger opportunity in my estimation."
>
> Moe has worked for almost fifteen years at converting the K–12 education system into a cash cow for Wall Street. A veteran of Lehman Brothers and Merrill Lynch, he now leads an investment group that specializes in raising money for businesses looking to tap into more than $1 trillion in taxpayer money spent annually on primary education. His consortium of wealth management and consulting firms, called Global Silicon Valley Partners, helped K12 Inc. (a for-profit online charter school) go public and has advised a number of other education companies in finding capital.
>
> Moe's conference marked a watershed moment in school privatization. His first Education Innovation Summit, held last year, attracted about 370 people and fifty-five presenting companies. This year, his conference hosted more than 560 people and 100 companies, and featured luminaries like former DC Mayor Adrian Fenty and former New York

City schools chancellor Joel Klein, now an education executive at News Corporation, a recent high-powered entrant into the for-profit education field (Ravitch 2013, 188).

Largest charter school chain

It will come as a surprise to many, if not most, people that the largest chain of charter schools in the United States is affiliated with a reclusive imam who lives in rural Pennsylvania and commands a powerful political organization in Turkey (Ravitch 2013, 166). This chain is called the Gulen Charter Schools.

In a special report entitled "The Gulen Movement" which aired on May 13, 2012, CBS News correspondent Lesley Stahl reported that, over the past decade, scores of charter schools have popped up all over the United States. They are founded and largely run by immigrants from Turkey who are carrying out the teachings of a Turkish Islamic cleric named Fethullah Gulen.

Gulen, she explained, is the spiritual leader of a growing and increasingly influential force in the Muslim world known as "The Gulen Movement," with millions upon millions of disciples who compare him to Gandhi and Martin Luther King. She reported that Gulen promotes tolerance, interfaith dialogue, and, above all, education.

According to the online encyclopedia, Wikipedia, the Gulen movement has private and charter schools in more than 140 countries. The movement also has substantial investments in media, finance, and for-profit health clinics.

In the United States, as of 2013, there were nearly 140 Gulen charter schools in sixteen states. These schools focus on mathematics and science and employ many Turkish teachers. Their corporate boards are usually made up entirely of Turkish men.

In Texas, which has one of highest concentration of Gulen charter schools in the United States, the *New York Times* reported that the three dozen Gulen schools there received $100 million annually in public funding and "had granted millions of dollars in construction and renovation contracts to firms run by Turkish-Americans with ties to the Gulen movement" (Ravitch 2013, 166).

White Hat Management

In Ohio, state law does not permit for-profit corporations to own and operate a charter school. However, state law permits the board of a nonprofit charter school to hire a for-profit company to manage it.

White Hat Management is the largest charter school management company in the state. White Hat is owned by Akron businessman David Brennan and operates fifty charter schools in six states. Thirty of the schools are in Ohio.

Brennan is a powerful figure in Ohio politics. He and his family have donated millions of dollars to Ohio's politicians, and lobbyists for White Hat have played a significant role in writing charter legislation. From 2001 to 2010, he donated nearly $3 million to political candidates running for public office (Ravitch 2013, 196).

Misgivings about Ohio's charter schools were conveyed in an editorial published in the *Toledo Blade*:

> When charter schools emerged on the Ohio educational scene more than a decade ago, they were hailed by many, including this newspaper, as a potentially innovative and lower-cost alternative to the state's disturbingly mediocre public school system. What was not envisioned is that charter schools—officially known as community schools— would become cash repositories to be siphoned of sponsorship and management fees, in some cases by politically connected individuals (*Toledo Blade* 2006).

Since 1999, White Hat Management has received nearly

$1 billion from the state of Ohio to operate its charter schools (Ravitch 2013, 169).

Cyberschooling

Cyberschooling in K–12 education is big business. By 2012, there were more than 200,000 full-time students enrolled in online charter schools in the United States (Ravitch 2013, 182).

Even though they receive less funding per student than traditional brick-and-mortar schools, cyberschooling is very profitable because there are no school buildings. Online charter schools do not have to pay for custodians, heating and cooling costs, libraries, gymnasiums, guidance counselors, playgrounds, after-school activities, and transportation.

Founded in 2000, K12 Inc. enrolled 100,000 students by 2012 and was recognized as our nation's largest company in cyberschooling. Publicly traded on the New York Stock Exchange, K12 Inc. reported revenues that year of nearly three quarters of a billion dollars. According to an analysis by the *New York Times* in 2010, K12 spent $26.5 million on advertising—all of which was funded with public dollars (Ravitch 2013, 182).

By 2015, the cyberschooling industry is projected to generate about $25 billion. Notably, all of the money will come from the tax dollars used to educate children in charter schools (Berliner and Glass 2014, 34).

A corporate takeover in progress

While there is much more evidence I could share about the privatization of our nation's public schools, I am going to resist the temptation to put you to sleep with more facts, figures, and case studies. Instead, I will stop and hope that I have already provided enough evidence to make a case for the major point of this chapter—and it is this: Until now, many people who saw that a corporate takeover of our nation's schools might be occurring were concerned that they would be viewed as conspiracy theorists. As a result, no one spoke up and raised a red warning flag about what was occurring.

Today, however, thanks to the research conducted by Diane Ravitch, David Berliner, Gene Glass, and other historians, it has become clear that today's education reform movement is not focusing on just reforming public education. Instead, it is blatantly working to leverage the power of our government to replace public education with a privately managed, free-market system of schooling.

As a result, America's schools are at a turning point. In the next three chapters, I explain how the education reform movement is impacting both our children and our teachers and why we, the people, have been sitting back and doing nothing about the situation.

References

Berliner, David C. and Gene V. Glass. 2014. *50 Myths & Lies That Threaten America's Public Schools: The Real Crisis in Education.* New York: Columbia University Teachers College Press.

Ravitch, Diane. 2010. *Life and Death of the Great American School System: How Testing and Choice Are Undermining Education.* New York: Basic Books.

Ravitch, Diane. 2013. *Reign of Error: The Hoax of the Privatization Movement and the Danger to America's Public Schools.* New York: Alfred A. Knopf.

"A Political Education." *Toledo Blade.* 2006, July 9. Editorial page writers. http://www.toledoblade.com/Editorials/2006/07/10/A-political-education.html.

Part II

The Impact of Education Reform

Good intentions can have unintended consequences. While the education reform movement may have been built upon a foundation of good intentions, the unintended consequences of education reform are creating a number of serious challenges that need to be discussed and addressed by the American people.

Chapter 6

Over-Testing Our Children

In many aspects of life, there are often two sides to a story. When it comes to education reform, there is both an upside and a downside for our children.

The upside is that the work being done to teach them high-level thinking skills is beginning to pay off. Based upon early anecdotal reports from superintendents and teachers with whom I work, their students are already demonstrating their innate ability to problem-solve and think creatively.

"This year, my students' understanding of math concepts has improved," stated an elementary school teacher from Ohio. "For me, the biggest plus of the Common Core Standards is that they increase the determination of many of our students to learn. By equipping them with tools and strategies aligned with these new standards to solve complex math problems, for example, they don't give up when they get stuck."

The downside of the education reform movement is that our children are being over-tested in math and language arts. As a result, other school subjects are receiving less emphasis because too much time is being spent teaching students how to pass these high-stakes tests.

High-level thinking

It has been well-documented that children are equipped with the ability to problem-solve and think creatively long before they start going to school. From a very early age, they find creative ways to demonstrate both creativity and problem solving.

The importance of teaching high-level thinking skills to our students has been on the radar screen of many of our public schools for the past decade. With the introduction of the Common Core Standards, our educational policymakers have served notice that teaching our students these thinking skills now needs to be on everyone's radar screen.

The good news is that the hard work of our teachers appears to be making a difference. The following quote from a teacher in one southern Arizona school district resonates with what I am hearing from many other teachers:

> Students are not only achieving at a higher level, but also taking responsibility for their learning. Throughout the year, I have had parents question why I was teaching certain things such as rules for discussions, temporal words, commas in a series, progressive nouns, and missing numbers in equations. It is encouraging to not only point out that they are part of the first grade standards but that many students are being successful at reaching this higher level of academic expectations (Nogales 2014).

As I have stated previously, the problem with the Common Core Standards is not the widely supported goal of teaching our students high level thinking skills. Rather, the problem rests with the accountability system that has been created to reach this goal.

In their zeal to make sure our teachers and our schools are held accountable for successfully implementing the Common Core

Standards, our education policymakers have increased the focus on high-stakes testing and are utilizing this testing to evaluate both our teachers and our schools. As a result, our children are being over-tested.

Over-testing

On April 2, 2014, a reporter for the *Washington Post* published a powerful letter from the teachers of a public secondary school in New York City regarding their concerns about the over-testing of America's children. The following slightly edited excerpts from that letter capture the essence of what they had to say:

> When they enter our school each fall, our sixth-graders write about their hopes and fears for middle school. This year, 35 percent said their greatest fear was failing the state tests. At one of the most socially difficult times of their lives, over a third of our children have more anxiety about standardized tests than any other issue.
>
> What has happened?
>
> This year in our school, as in schools across the country, we have seen the number of standardized tests we are required to administer grow sharply, from 25 to more than 50 (in grades 6–10). In the next six weeks alone, each of our sixth-graders will be required to take 18 days of tests: three days of state English tests, three days of state math tests, four days of new city English and math benchmark tests, and eight days of new English, math, social studies, and science city tests to evaluate teacher performance.
>
> Additionally, students who are learning English must spend two to three more days taking the NYSESLAT test for English Language Learners—a total of 21 days in just the next few weeks.
>
> One teacher at our school asked her seventh-graders

how they felt about the tests. "I feel nervous," said one, "because you think you're not going to pass." Another protested, "I don't think tests show our learning, and they don't show our growth." A third stated, "It makes it more possible to fail."

Let us be clear at the outset. As a staff, we are not opposed to all standardized tests and believe that, used sparingly, such tests can provide useful feedback to schools, teachers, and possibly students. We are instead concerned about their vast and increasing number and—just as disconcerting—outsized influence.

The tests are no longer about feedback. The stakes attached to them now commonly include school funding and evaluation and closure, teacher pay and evaluation and firings, and of course, student promotion and self-perception. It should come as no surprise that many schools have chosen to focus more and more of the school year on what is often called test prep.

This week, as our school enters another season of testing, our sixth- and eighth-grade teachers have chosen to read to students a principal's letter that one parent posted online: "We are concerned that these tests do not always assess all of what it is that make each of you special and unique . . . the scores you get will tell you something, but they will not tell you everything. There are many ways of being smart."

Our students spontaneously cheered. That they could be seen as individuals with interests and friends and dreams—not just as a set of numbers—deeply resonated with them. (Strauss 2014)

Teachers are not alone in their concern about over-testing. One parent who had recently moved to the South from the Northeast explained that she had her first glimpse at the "testing madness" when her children were in kindergarten. For weeks leading up to the end of their kindergarten year, she said their classrooms were essentially on lockdown while some students took end-of-grade exams and others (kindergarteners included) took field tests for another testing endeavor. She added that while there was no art, gym, and music, and only a limited amount of time for recess, sadly, there was a lot of stress.

By a 57 percent to 29 percent margin, parents of public school children said in an American Federation of Teachers national poll that there is too much testing, and 57 percent said testing has taken away too much time from teaching and learning (AFT 2014).

A case study of two school districts

A close examination of standardized testing in 2013 by the American Federation of Teachers found that students are losing out on receiving a full, high-quality education because of test preparation and testing. *Testing More, Teaching Less: What America's Obsession with Student Testing Costs in Money and Lost Instructional Time* explores the instructional and financial costs of testing in 2012–13 in two medium-sized, urban school districts—one located in the Midwest, the other in the East (Nelson 2013). "The current accountability system has led districts to fixate on testing and sanctions, has squeezed out vital parts of the curriculum that are not subject to testing, and has sacrificed much-needed learning time," stated AFT president Randi Weingarten. "That is not what high-performing countries do, and it is not what the United States should do."

In the Midwestern school district, nineteen days out of a school year were devoted to test preparation and testing. Students in grades 3–10 spent at least fifteen hours—or three school days—taking state-mandated tests, interim benchmarking tests, and other academic assessments. Students in grades 3–8 spent at least sixty hours—or sixteen school days—preparing for state-mandated tests, the associated interim benchmarking tests, and other district assessments.

In the Eastern school district, six weeks out of the school year are devoted to test prep and testing. Students in grades 6–11 spent up to fifty hours—or two weeks—taking state-mandated tests, interim benchmarking tests, and other district academic assessments. The district also devoted 110 hours or more—about one month of the school year—to test preparation.

In addition to lost instructional time, the financial impact of standardized testing was significant for both school districts. The Midwestern school district's annual cost of testing per pupil in grades 3–8 was $600 or more. For grades K–2, testing costs were around $200 per student. In high school, except for grade twelve, per-student testing costs ranged from $400 to $600.

The Eastern school district's annual cost of per pupil testing in grades 6–11 exceeded $1,100. For grades 1–2, testing costs were $400 per student, and for grades 3–5, costs ranged from $700 to $800 per pupil.

The AFT report suggested that redirected time and money devoted to excessive testing could be used to focus on problem-solving and critical-thinking skills and restore subjects not tested and/or that have been cut, such as art, music, physical education, and foreign languages. The financial savings also could be used to purchase the high-stakes tests aligned to the Common Core State Standards which are predicted to cost between $20 and $35 more per test-taker than the current $20 per test-taker in a typical state.

Teaching to the test

The impact that education reform is having on our children involves more than just the time they spend and stress they experience taking high-stakes tests. It also includes the time being devoted to preparing them for these tests.

As a consequence of the enormous pressure being placed upon teachers to raise their students' scores on high-stakes tests, some teachers are providing classroom instruction which includes as practice activities the actual items on the tests. Other teachers are giving practice exercises featuring items that are similar to the test's actual items. In either case, these teachers are teaching to the test.

A first-grade teacher in Arizona shares her perspective of the impact of teaching to the test: "I think that the goals of the Common Core Standards are good, and I truly believe they were created with the students' best interests at heart. However, in trying to implement these new standards, it seems that all we are doing is teaching to another test. We are teaching students so many different strategies that sometimes we seem to confuse them rather than help them."

With some schools allocating up to 20 percent of the school year to preparing their students for state tests, the big question for me is: Does all of this focus on test preparation improve student learning?

Although I am not a teacher, I have asked many teachers with whom I work this important question. And here is what they have told me. Standardized tests are, by definition, tests removed from student engagement and context and require a particular kind of teaching that is antithetical to what most teachers believe education should be. While educational standards, including the Common Core, are a central part of our curriculum work, they are only one of many considerations embedded in the work our students do.

Teaching to the test typically means to teach without context or commitment and without personal connection or application. It means to teach using excerpted writing passages and scripted questions.

In contrast to being taught to the test, students produce better work when they believe it is meaningful and connects with real world issues and concerns. These issues and concerns can range from bullying in their school and their student dress code to challenges and opportunities facing their community. Students may spend weeks on a single case study, developing nuanced understandings of these complex problems. In this work, they are evaluated by school-based assessments which, in contrast to high-stakes standardized tests, take the shape of diverse projects and presentations.

Some teachers also believe that the emphasis on testing takes away time from teaching critical-thinking and problem-solving skills. Steven Weinberg, a teacher on special assignment in Oakland, California, where a major part of his job is "helping teachers teach to the test," says: "The trouble with teaching to the test is that the standardized tests are not, by their nature, able to measure meaningful learning and emphasize the trivial rather than the essential." He continues:

> Take, for example, writing. Instead of measuring how well students can express themselves clearly, the tests ask students to select the best wording from four choices, often written about a topic that the students are not familiar with. As teachers prepare students for this kind of test, they are encouraged to forego having students actually write compositions, in favor of practicing multiple-choice test prep. In history, the emphasis is on specific facts rather than historical understanding. In math and science, deep understanding is sacrificed for coverage.
> (GreatSchools 2014).

In the opinion of GreatSchools, a national nonprofit organization based in Oakland, California, and a leading provider of school performance information for parents, the positive or negative impact of teaching to the test depends upon the test and the teacher (GreatSchools 2014). If the test measures the skills students are expected to be learning, and teachers prepare students by teaching those skills, then teaching to the test is a good thing.

But if the test is not directly related to what is being taught or teachers depend on repeated drills with old test questions to prepare students, it is a different story. Teaching to the test can waste valuable learning time.

Finland's approach to testing

Finland's education system has consistently scored at or near the top in international test scores. Education testing policies in Finland, however, are very different from policies that drive education in the United States.

In Finland, teachers are respected, and students don't take a mountain of standardized tests. In fact, they take only one high-stakes standardized test. It is called the National Matriculation Examination.

Paul Sahlberg, a visiting professor at the Harvard Graduate School of Education and former director general of Finland's Ministry of Education, explains his country's approach to educating its students:

> Many Americans who visit Finland to examine its education system are surprised by how rarely students are required to take standardized tests during their twelve years of schooling. They learn that students are primarily assessed by multiple teacher-made tests that vary from one school to another. At the national level, sample-based student assessments similar to the National Assessment of Educational Progress that have no stakes for students, teachers, or schools are the main means to inform policy-makers and the public on how Finland's school system is performing. Teachers and principals in Finland have a strong sense of professional responsibility to teach their children well but

also to judge how well children have learned what they are supposed to learn according to a curriculum designed by teachers (Strauss 2014).

An important lesson

More than a decade ago, I learned an important lesson from a government teacher about why narrowing the focus of teaching and learning is a problem. He explained to me that there are many reasons why children are motivated to do well in school. For some children, it is math or science or social studies. For others, it is art or music or an extracurricular activity.

The point he was making is that when a student has a favorite subject and does well in it, that student is likely to not just tolerate but often do well in other school subjects. So, every time a subject gets scaled back or is eliminated, some students lose the connection which motivates them to learn or even stay in school.

One of the unintended consequences of the educational standards movement during the past two decades and the current over-testing of our children is that our public schools have had to narrow their educational focus. To comply with these new standards, our teachers are having to spend an inordinate amount of time and energy preparing our children for high-stakes tests in math and language arts and less time on the other subjects that are important and matter to our students.

In the next chapter, I document how the cumulative effect of having to comply with years of education reform is impacting our teachers and that, as a result, they are being stretched to their breaking point.

References

AFT. 2014, July 23. "Testing More, Teaching Less: What America's Obsession with Student Testing Costs in Money and

Lost Instructional Time." Press release from the American Federation of Teachers. http://www.aft.org/newspubs/press/2013/072313.cfm.

GreatSchools. 2014. "What's So Bad About Teaching to the Test?" http://www.greatschools.org/students/academic-skills/400-teaching-to-the-test.gs.

Nelson, Howard. 2013. "Testing More, Teaching Less: What America's Obsession with Student Testing Costs in Money and Lost Instructional Time." Washington, DC: American Federation of Teachers.

Nogales 2014. Quote provided anonymously by a teacher in the Nogales Unified School District, Nogales, Arizona.

Strauss, Valerie. 2014. "The Brainy Questions on Finland's Only High-stakes Standardized Test." The Answer Sheet, March 24. http://www.washingtonpost.com/blogs/answer-sheet/wp/2014/03/24/the-brainy-questions-on-finlands-only-high-stakes-standardized-test/.

_____. 2014, April 2. "Is Testing Taking Over Our Schools? An Entire Faculty Answers." *Washington Post*.

Chapter 7

Overwhelming Our Teachers

As you read in chapter 6, the hard work being done by our teachers to implement the goals of the Common Core Standards is beginning to pay off. In a number of school districts, students are demonstrating they can master the kinds of high-level thinking skills that are required in today's world.

The big question, however, is this: can this initial success be sustained? Currently, the answer is very much up in the air.

The harsh reality

The harsh reality is that our teachers are overwhelmed by the parade of education reforms being foisted onto them and their students. Many of our teachers are worn out both physically and emotionally, and some are being stretched to their breaking point. I see it occurring every day in my work, and it is not just a result of the pressure being placed on them by the recently mandated Common Core Standards.

The morale of America's teachers has been negatively impacted by multiple waves of school reform since the Reagan Administration published *A Nation at Risk* in 1983. One of the reasons for the drop in morale is that education reformers have frequently charged that teachers were failing to do their jobs properly and competently and will not work hard unless their livelihoods are threatened (Dworkin 2008, 119).

An all-too-common example of how waves of school reform efforts have negatively impacted teacher morale is contained in the heartfelt words of a twenty-four-year veteran teacher in Ohio. On March 3, 2014, she posted the following letter on the newspaper website of the *Washington Post*:

> It isn't even 6:30 at night, but I'm done. I already have my pajamas on and don't have the energy to do one productive thing all evening. I drove home after an after-school meeting (looking at student test data) tonight feeling a bit sorry for myself since this is my least favorite time of the school year . . . the countdown to the big Ohio Achievement Assessment (OAA) which is the end-all, be-all in the Ohio world of education.
>
> Our fifth-graders have learned so much this year. Most of them can write a seven-paragraph essay in one sitting. They have read novel after novel after novel. They know what plot events are, credible sources, hyperbole, onomatopoeia, and how an author arranged a nonfiction piece of writing. They've studied Rosa Parks, Robert Frost, Lucretia Mott, Abraham Lincoln, Garrett Morgan, Emily Dickinson, Nelson Mandela, Helen Keller, MLK, Winston Churchill, Gandhi, Cesar Chavez, etc. (over thirty biographies in all). We've "been to" England, Mexico, Ireland, Denmark, and Japan during our school studies. It has been an exciting, fun, whirlwind year, and I love these kids. This has been one of my favorite groups of students ever.
>
> We could do SO MUCH with this foundation now. More of them could become published. (I just dropped off some of their editorials to the newspaper today.) More of them could participate in creative contests. (One student

was just chosen to go to a table decorating contest based on the "healthy sandwich" she designed.) We could invite community leaders in for a luncheon and help develop their activist spirit. We could do a cultural fair and invite the younger students in our building to come and learn from us. We could get OUT of the building and visit local businesses so our students could see firsthand why their education matters. (You know, the things I USED to do in education, even once taking my students on a flying field trip.)

But what do we have to do now? Test Prep.

And why do we have to do it? Because no matter how fluent my students are, no matter how amazing their writing, no matter how much they know about so many topics, they MUST be able to sit for two and a half hours straight and read 6–7 reading selections and write approximately 12 essay questions giving the scorers EXACTLY what they're looking for or they won't get their points and they won't get their scores. And since they're going off to middle school next year, I want them to start with the highest "label" they can get (because with these tests, students DO get labeled, and the state is the biggest "label lover" of them all).

Oh, and let's not forget that after taking the Ohio Achievement Assessments reading test on Monday, the students will then take the math test on Wednesday, and then the science test on Friday. Three days of testing = 7 1/2 hours of testing. For 10- and 11-year-old students. (The third and fourth graders will be testing for five hours in one week.) Wow. Just . . . wow. I just heard today that next year, students may be taking these same tests in March AND May. Now, won't that just be double the fun? Be still my heart.

And do we get the graded tests back? No! We get

"scores" but no graded tests. And have there been reports from past test scorers that some of the scoring isn't ethical or honest or well done? Yes! So do I TRUST the scoring? No. Why aren't parents DEMANDING to see their students' graded tests from the state? I don't know.

One past test expected a sixth-grader to know what "third-person omniscient" was. Really?! If a student vomits on a test, we DO have to put the sealed test in a plastic bag and send it back to the state. Apparently, a teacher isn't trustworthy enough to give her word that there was a student, there was vomit, and now there is a non-scorable test. I'll have my plastic gloves on the front table before we begin.

I have to TEACH my students to write in a specific way just for this OAA test. Yes, for this ONE test on this one day in their lives, which will give them a "label" of their knowledge (limited, basic, proficient, accelerated, advanced), which is supposed to represent their entire school year with me.

And I'll get my label, too, based on their label. From my school district. From my state. For my life.

For tonight, my label is "Fed Up." I just want to teach. I just want to make learning come alive for my students. I just want to make a difference. But tomorrow, I will go into school with a big smile on my face and motivate my students to jump through hoops so they can go on to middle school ready to pass any test thrown their way. And I'll make it fun, and we'll laugh, and I'll do whatever I can to try to make it my students' fondest year yet.

But I have to tell you, school just isn't for children anymore" (*Strauss and Neely-Randall* 2014).

This plea for help resonates with what I am hearing from many other teachers in the schools where I work. Like her, they are physically exhausted and emotionally demoralized from the unreasonable demands and growing pressure being placed on them.

Speaking out like this, however, is not typical for most teachers because there is an unwritten rule within the teaching profession that if you are a teacher, you don't complain. Whatever happens to you, you go along with it, do your job with a smile on your face, and then try to figure out how to make it work.

Unfortunately, this unwritten rule is problematic because it creates the illusion that everything is fine and hides important challenges facing our schools that need to be addressed. One of those challenges is the increasing pressure being placed on the backs of our teachers.

The teacher burnout problem

The results of the twenty-eighth annual MetLife Survey of the American Teacher provide a clear look at the price our education system is paying for this growing pressure. They indicate that the percentage of teachers who said they were thinking of leaving the profession within the next five years increased from 17 percent in 2009 to 29 percent in 2012 (Heitin 2012).

The graph on the next page shows that teacher job satisfaction declined by 23 percent between 2008 and 2012 (Harris Interactive 2013):

Percentage of teachers who say they are very satisfied with their jobs

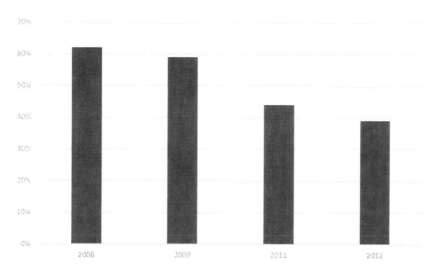

The MetLife Survey of the American Teacher: Challenges for School Leadership, p. 45.

In addition, the MetLife survey found that more than half (51 percent) of our teachers today say they are experiencing great stress either almost every day or several days of the week. In 1985, the percentage of teachers experiencing this level of stress was about one out of three (36 percent).

One of the consequences of this growing level of stress is that the number of years of teaching experience in our public schools is dropping significantly. According to *Education Week*, the most frequent number of years that American teachers have been on the job has decreased from fifteen years in 1987–88 to just one year in 2007–08. While inexperienced teachers can provide high energy and a fresh perspective, it can take up to five years or more for them to become seasoned teaching professionals. To be most effective, teaching staffs need to include a balanced blend of new and experienced teachers.

So, how widespread is the teacher burnout problem and the loss of some of our brightest and most highly regarded educators? The answer is that some school systems are better able than others to cushion their teachers from the overwhelming impact of education reform.

Generally speaking, high-wealth, low-poverty school districts with strong local financial support are better able to help their teachers navigate the rough waters of education reform than are low-wealth, high-poverty districts. The reason is that financially stable school districts often have more flexibility. They have more teachers and educational support staff to shoulder the burden of trying to sustain current initiatives that are working while meeting the demands of new education reform mandates.

A high-achieving, financially stable school district in northeast Ohio serves as a good example of the importance of having this kind of flexibility. Thanks to its strong financial condition, the district had provided its teachers with a significant amount of high-quality staff development and, as a result, was able to modify its successful reading program to meet the state's newly imposed Third Grade Reading Guarantee standard. Even though teachers in the district experienced some frustration as a result of the mandated shift in policy, they were able to incorporate the new reading standards into their teaching with a minimum amount of wasted energy and lost effort.

Low-wealth, high-poverty school systems, on the other hand, are often highly dependent upon state support and find it difficult, if not impossible, to build enough educational capacity and flexibility to effectively build on successful past initiatives while meeting new education reform mandates. In these districts, the burden of trying to do everything with minimal support falls on the backs of a limited number of teachers and support staff.

Despite the growing pressure

Even though many of our teachers are physically exhausted and emotionally demoralized by the weight of our nation's education reform movement, they continue to place the educational needs of their students ahead of themselves. They continue to push forward in trying to meet the growing expectations being placed upon them.

The results of a recent survey of teachers conducted in a suburban school district in northeast Ohio (Staff Survey Report 2013) illustrate this point.

When asked what they felt was the greatest challenge facing them, the number-one response of the teachers in the Avon Local School District was keeping up with the never-ending changes coming at them and the lack of time for them to do what is expected of them. They said they need more time for professional development, student instruction, and collaboration with other teachers. As one teacher stated, "For some of us, the stress level is through the roof."

Another teacher summed up what I believe many other teachers in our country are feeling today: "We all want to do the best we can, but the lack of time and increasing pressure on top of what have always been high-demand, high-pressure positions make it feel next to impossible to succeed."

Despite the growing pressure and frustration being felt by many teachers in the Avon Local Schools, they are not wavering in their support of the Common Core Standards. They believe these educational standards are good for their students because they promote a deep understanding of topics and help students engage in high-order thinking.

What's more, this is not an isolated point of view. It is how the vast majority of teachers with whom I come into contact feel. And based upon a recent nationwide study, it resonates with how the vast majority of teachers throughout our country feel. In the study, superintendents from nearly every state in our nation indicated that their staff are prepared and engaged in implementing the new standards. In addition, the study reported that several separate surveys show that teachers, overall, are very supportive of the new standards (Finanan 2014).

Three major concerns

However, no matter how committed they may be to turning the Common Core Standards into a success story for their students, our teachers are not machines. They are human beings who have limits on the amount of pressure and change they can be expected to tolerate.

Because our teachers can tolerate only so much, I have three major concerns moving forward. One is that our education policymakers will continue to pressure our teachers to perform unrealistic feats of heroism and push many more of them to the point where they say, enough is enough, and they decide to leave the teaching profession.

My second major concern is that the unrealistic implementation timelines and testing currently in place for meeting the goals of the Common Core Standards will trigger a significant drop in student test scores. These falling test scores then will reinforce the charges by many education reformers that our public schools are failing and need to be replaced by a more efficient and effective free market-based education system.

Thirdly, if the historical pattern of school reform in our nation follows its normal course, there is a good chance that the Common Core Standards will ultimately get derailed and be replaced by another top-down mandate by our country's education policymakers to "fix our failing schools." If this occurs, our teachers will be told one more time to shift gears, abandon much of what they are currently doing in the classroom, and pour their heart and soul into a new way to save our country from our nation's "underperform-ing" education system.

References

Dworkin, Anthony Gary. 2008. "School Reform and Teacher Burnout." In *Schools and Society: A Sociological Approach to Education*, edited by Jeanne H. Ballantine and Joan Z. Spade. Thousand Oaks, CA: Pine Forge Press.

Finanan, Leslie. 2014. "Common Core and Other State Standards: Superintendents Feel Optimism, Concern and Lack of Support." Alexandria, VA: The School Superintendents' Association.

Harris Interactive. 2013. "The MetLife Survey of the American Teacher: Challenges for School Leadership."

Heitin, Liana. 2012, March 7. "Survey: Teacher Job Satisfaction Hits a Low Point" *Education Week*.

Staff Survey Report (2013, February), Executive Summary, Avon Local School District, Avon, Ohio. A copy of the complete survey report is available at the administrative offices of the Board of Education of the Avon Local School District, 35573 Detroit Road, Avon, Ohio 44011.

Strauss, Valerie and Dawn Neely-Randall. 2014, March 3. "Why school isn't for children anymore—teacher," *Washington Post*.

Chapter 8

Undermining Support for Our Schools

As a result of being told by education reformers that our nation's education system is failing us, it is becoming increasingly difficult to generate state and local support for our public schools. For example, from 2008 to 2013, state funding for our public schools was reduced in thirty-seven states. The graph (figure 1) on the next page shows the percentage of change in financial support for all fifty states.

Because of these reductions in state funding, school officials in most states are having to turn to their local communities for financial support. In forty-one of our fifty states, this support for our schools is contingent upon the passage of local school tax initiatives (Ballotpedia 2014).

Missouri, for example, mandates school bond and tax elections if a school district wants to issue new bonding for capital improvements and new construction or exceed the tax rate of a basic operating levy. Missouri also has tough supermajority requirements. A bond issue requires a four-sevenths passage vote (57.15 percent) while any referendum involving exceeding the operating levy cap requires a two-thirds supermajority vote (66.7 percent) for approval.

Figure 1

Per-student Spending Has Decreased In Most States Since 2008

Percent change in spending per student, inflation-adjusted, FY08 to FY13

State	Percent change
Arizona	-21.8%
Alabama	-21.7%
Oklahoma	-20.3%
Idaho	-19.0%
South Carolina	-18.0%
California*	-17.3%
Georgia	-14.8%
Wisconsin	-13.7%
North Carolina	-13.7%
South Dakota	-13.6%
Kansas	-13.2%
Mississippi	-12.9%
Oregon	-12.8%
Illinois	-11.3%
Texas	-11.2%
New Mexico	-10.8%
Virginia	-10.0%
Colorado	-9.4%
Maine	-8.8%
Michigan	-8.8%
Kentucky	-8.5%
Utah	-8.1%
Ohio	-7.9%
Florida	-7.4%
Arkansas	-5.3%
Nevada	-3.9%
Washington	-2.8%
Missouri	-2.3%
Vermont	-1.3%
Pennsylvania	-1.2%
Nebraska	-1.1%
Louisiana	-1.0%
Minnesota	-1.0%
New Jersey	-0.8%
New York	-0.1%
Tennessee	0.9%
Delaware	0.9%
Montana	1.0%
West Virginia	1.4%
Rhode Island	2.7%
New Hampshire	4.6%
Wyoming	5.1%
Connecticut	6.1%
Massachusetts	6.7%
Alaska	6.7%
Maryland	7.4%
Iowa	10.6%
North Dakota	28.2%

*California data are based on the 2012-13 state budget as enacted. This enacted budget includes anticipated revenues from Proposition 30, a measure that will appear on the November 2012 statewide ballot.

Sources: CBPP budget analysis and National Center for Education Statistics enrollment estimates.

Center on Budget and Policy Priorities | cbpp.org

Wisconsin has a revenue cap which limits the amount of property tax revenue school districts can collect. If a school district wants to exceed its revenue limit, it is required to have a ballot measure. Wisconsin also requires ballot measures for any school bonding that exceeds a million dollars.

In Indiana, a ballot measure is required for school districts to exceed the property tax revenue limit, issue new bonding for new construction or capital improvements, or issue new property taxes to pay the mandatory excess property tax credit. Indiana sets strict time frames on elections. For example, if a referendum is defeated, school districts have to wait one year before restarting the process of issuing a ballot question to the district's voters.

The difficulty of passing a tax increase

While the rules for local school tax initiatives vary from state to state, all of these initiatives have one thing in common. When they involve an increase in taxes, they are difficult to pass.

In Ohio, for example, the passage rate is only about 40 percent for school issues proposing an increase in taxes. Proposals to renew existing taxes, however, fare much better. Nearly 90 percent of them are approved by Ohio's voters.

An analysis of the election results in fifteen states by Ballotpedia, an online encyclopedia about American politics and elections, shows that 72.1 percent of the voters in these states approved local school bond and tax measure proposals for their schools in 2012. [http://ballotpedia.org/Approval_rates_of_local_school_bond_and_tax_elections_(2012)] While at first glance, it may appear that these results contradict Ohio's findings, it is important to point out that these results included both tax increases and renewals. The states involved in the study were Arizona, California, Colorado, Florida, Illinois, Michigan, Missouri, New Mexico, New Jersey, New York, Ohio, Oregon, Texas, Washington, and Wisconsin.

The impact on parents

The education reform movement is also undermining parental support. For example, newly-published research from the University of Massachusetts Amherst shows that parents of public school students in states with more extensive and stringent student assessment systems express lower trust in government, less confidence in government efficacy, and more negative views of their children's schools.

In this study published by the journal *Political Behavior*, associate professor Jesse Rhodes found that highly developed school testing and assessment policies alienate parents from government and discourage parental involvement in education (Rhodes 2014, 1). He discovered that parental trust in government was 11 percent lower in states with the most extensive school assessment policies and parental views of government effectiveness were 15 percent lower compared to states with less developed testing policies and procedures.

Rhodes also found that parents in states with more developed assessment systems were less likely to contact teachers, participate in school fundraisers, and get involved in other parental involvement activities. The likelihood that parents would contact their children's teachers was 17 percent lower in states with the most stringent testing policies and the chance they would participate in school fundraisers was 28 percent lower.

"My findings suggest that a major reassessment of standards, testing, and accountability policies is necessary," Rhodes concludes. "At a minimum, standards-based reforms must be redesigned so that they engage parents more directly in the process of policy design and administration and allay parental concerns about counter-productive consequences" (Science Daily 2014).

The erosion of parental support and the added pressure on

local taxpayers to offset reductions in state funding are increasing the need to pass local school tax initiatives. In the next chapter, I explain why many of the campaigns being waged to pass these initiatives are so disruptive and, as a result, are dividing our communities.

References

Rhodes, Jesse. 2014, March 14. "Learning Citizenship? How State Education Reforms Affect Parents' Attitudes and Behavior." *Political Behavior*.

University of Massachusetts Amherst. 2014. "Education: States' standardized tests have a negative impact on parents' civic engagement." *ScienceDaily*. www.sciencedaily.com/releases/2014/04/140407130927.htm.

Chapter 9

Dividing Our Communities

Another unintended consequence of education reform is the way in which undermining support for our public schools is dividing our communities by pitting citizens against one another in campaigns to pass local school tax initiatives.

As someone who has spent the past twenty-five years working with schools and communities seeking public support for school tax issues, I discovered early in my career that the campaigns being waged to pass these school tax issues can be very divisive. More often than not, they pit citizens (yes voters and no voters) against one another and, in the process, inflict a great amount of emotional damage upon a community. Unfortunately, in my experience, this is the rule rather than the exception.

Throughout my career, I have been trying to figure out how to minimize the damage being incurred by these divisive school tax initiatives. In doing so, I have repeatedly asked myself the basic question: Why is this happening and what is the root cause of the problem?

What I have discovered is that, in the vast majority of instances, the public is not involved in the decision to place the school tax issue on the ballot. That decision is usually made in isolation by the school district's board of education.

As a result, in addition to not having any ownership in the decision to go on the ballot, most people in the community don't even understand why the schools need the money. It is not uncommon to hear community members say, "The schools ignore us until they need more money and then assume that we will give it to them. Then, if we say no, they keep coming back until we wear down and say yes."

In Ohio, for example, where I have conducted dozens of community opinion surveys and focus group discussions, school districts are allowed to place tax issues on the ballot four times a year. In a May primary or November general election, it is not unusual to have more than one hundred requests for money on the ballot in school districts throughout the state.

In addition, it is not uncommon for school districts to place the same tax issue on the ballot several times until it passes. I have worked in a number of districts where issues were rejected more than ten times in a row before they were approved. In these communities, levy fatigue and other side effects from constantly ignoring the will of the people and bombarding them with one tax issue request after another until they give in and say yes can be divisive, disruptive, and long lasting.

To make matters worse, the strategies that are often deployed to pass school tax issues insult our citizens and increase the tension in our communities. One of the favorite strategies used in school tax campaigns is to communicate only with the yes-voters and get them to the polls while ignoring the rest of the community with the hope that the no-voters will stay home.

This is a bad idea. Ignoring people says to them that you don't care about them and that they don't matter. In addition, this strategy divides our communities into good guys and bad guys— those who support our schools and those who do not. Later in the book, I share the anecdote for these highly divisive and unproductive strategies.

Additional unintended consequences

Voter disapproval of these disruptive school tax initiative campaigns are triggering a domino effect of negative, unintended consequences. One is the message that these defeats are sending to an already overburdened and demoralized teaching profession. That message is "Your community does not support you."

Another unintended consequence is the loss of high-quality students. When a community suffers through a series of tax initiative defeats, families began to move into other school districts or enroll their children in charter schools or private and parochial schools. Oftentimes, these students include some of the district's highest performers.

Finally, a community that develops the reputation for not supporting its public schools becomes a less inviting place in which to live. As a result, the school district is unable to attract young families and, over time, the community becomes stagnant. Ultimately, property values tumble, and everyone feels the effects of living in a divided community.

Chapter 10

Increasing Our Financial Burden

In addition to over-testing our children, overwhelming our teachers, undermining support for our schools, and dividing our communities, the time, energy, and money being spent trying to comply with the demands of the education reform movement are significantly increasing our nation's financial burden.

In February of 2012, the Pioneer Institute's Center for School Reform released an eye-opening national report revealing that implementing the Common Core Standards will generate at least $15.8 billion of new costs for states and local communities over the next seven years (Pioneer Institute, 2012). This increase in costs includes $1.2 billion for new assessments (high-stakes testing), $5.3 billion for professional development, $2.5 billion for textbooks and instructional materials, and $6.9 billion for technology and infrastructure support. The chart on the following page shows the total projected costs of implementing the Common Core Standards:

Fig. 2B. Projected Costs to Implement Common Core

	One Time	Year 1 Operations	Years 2–7 Ongoing Operations (Annual)	Total of One Time & 7 Operational Years
Testing Costs	$0	$177,234,471	$177,234,471	$1,240,641,297
Professional Development	$5,257,492,417	$0	$0	$5,257,492,417
Textbooks & Instructional Materials	$2,469,098,464	$0	$0	$2,469,098,464
Technology	$2,796,294,147	$326,042,312	$624,258,785	$6,867,889,169
TOTAL	$10,522,885,028	$503,276,783	$801,493,256	$15,835,121,347

Taken from the "National Cost of Aligning States and Localities to the Common Core Standards," Center for School Reform, Pioneer Institute, February, 2012, p. 2, Figure 2B.

At the local level, the taxpayers in one Ohio school district, for example, have spent more than a million dollars in educational supplies and materials to meet the requirements of the Common Core Standards. This is in addition to the time and energy being expended by the district's teachers and administrative staff. As the superintendent of that district explained, "The time and energy being wasted filling out useless forms, creating unnecessary reports, and providing staff development for practices and procedures that will likely change when the political winds shift direction is harder to quantify but is probably much more costly."

Diverting tax dollars to charter schools

Another consequence of the education reform movement is that our tax dollars are being diverted from our traditional public schools to charter schools. It is happening in school districts throughout our country and occurs when students leave their public school to attend a charter school and state funding for their public school district is transferred to the charter school in which they are enrolled.

On its website on March 19, 2014, the New York State School Boards Association alerted its members that state leaders were poised to divert hundreds of millions in critically needed funding for the public schools to the state's private, parochial, and charter schools.

In the state of Washington, the Washington Education Association reported that charter schools were diverting money and resources from the public schools. According to the association, forty publicly funded charter schools were projected over five years to drain up to $350 million from the state's traditional public schools.

In Texas, as I reported in chapter 5, three dozen Gulen charter schools were receiving $100 million annually in public funding.

According to the Ohio Department of Education, Ohio's public schools lost $800 million in state funding to charter schools in the Buckeye State in fiscal year 2013. In Lorain County, where the county's sixteen public districts lost $25 million to charter schools in 2013, each student in the county who leaves a public school to attend a charter school takes about $5,700 with him or her to that charter school.

In the 2012–2013 school year, half of the state funding for Ohio's charter schools went to schools that performed worse than the traditional public districts that students left behind. The state's charter schools also spent nearly twice as much—23.5 percent to

13 percent—on noninstructional administrative costs than did traditional public schools (Dyer 2014).

In addition to the loss of state funding to brick-and-mortar charter schools, our tax dollars are also being diverted from our public schools to virtual schools which operate under the same type of legal structure as traditional charter schools but provide full-time education entirely through online delivery into students' homes as opposed to a physical facility where students sit in classrooms and receive direct face-to-face instruction. As I noted in chapter 5, by 2015, the cyberschooling industry is projected to generate about $25 billion.

While I could provide more examples of how the education reform movement is increasing our nation's financial burden, I am going to stop short of flooding this chapter with additional statistics. Instead, I am going to hope that I have made the case that this burden is significant.

References

Dyer, Stephen. 2014. "Short-Changed: How Poor-Performing Charters Cost All Ohio Kids." Innovation Ohio, Columbus, Ohio. http://innovationohio.org/2014/04/22/report-over-half-of-ohios-charter-spending-goes-to-poor-performers/.

Pioneer Institute. 2012. "National Cost of Aligning States and Localities to the Common Core Standards." Boston, MA: Center for School Reform.

Chapter 11

Usurping Our Responsibility

Until I moved out of the comfort of my home and went to college, I was shielded by my mother from many of the important responsibilities of life. Although she was well-intentioned and helped mold my character in many positive ways, she controlled much of my thinking and resolved most of the problems I encountered.

For me, it was an easy life—at least for a while. Other than being expected to earn good grades in school, I really didn't have to do too much. When I needed money, I simply had to ask for it. Even when I participated in sports, my mother was there to provide me with an excuse when I needed one for why I wasn't a starter on the basketball team or didn't perform well in a particular game.

By enabling me to rely upon her for much of my existence during my formative years, she usurped my responsibility to begin the important journey of becoming a full-functioning, responsible adult.

Like my mother

The education reform movement is a little bit like my mother who did everything for me when I was young and enabled me to become irresponsible and dependent upon her. Like my mother who came to my rescue and fixed things for me when I needed help, education reformers have come to the rescue of our education system.

For the past three decades, they have been telling us that our public schools are failing but not to worry because "We'll fix them for you." Often with the best of intentions, many of our corporate leaders and education policymakers have usurped our responsibility for our schools and enabled us to become dependent upon them. And we, the American people, have allowed it to happen.

However, they are not alone. With the best of intentions, our country's local school officials have also inadvertently usurped our responsibility for our schools and enabled us to become dependent upon them. In fact, we are caught in a cross fire of enabling from both them and the leaders of our country's education reform movement.

Caught in a cross fire of enabling

While education reformers are telling us not to worry about our "failing schools" but just sit back and relax while "we fix them," we are being reassured by our local school officials that there is nothing to worry about—our schools are doing just fine. In their well-intentioned effort to provide effective leadership for our communities by accentuating the positive and downplaying the negative, they are unintentionally creating a false sense of security that everything is fine and obscuring major problems that need to be addressed.

Like my well-intentioned mother who did everything for me when I was young and enabled me to become irresponsible and dependent upon her, our local school officials and the leaders of the education reform movement are enabling us to be irresponsible and dependent upon them. So, while they are saying it in different ways, both our local school officials and leaders of our nation's education reform movement are usurping our responsibility by telling us that there is no need for us to get involved and do anything. And we are heeding their words.

Usurping our responsibility

There are a number of reasons why we are allowing our education policymakers to usurp our responsibility for our schools. One is that some of us are preoccupied with navigating the basic challenges of our daily lives while others are turned off by politics and don't want to get involved in anything that might appear to be political. Another reason why we are allowing it to happen is that some of us are simply lazy.

However, as I have learned over the years working with schools and communities, a significant segment of the American people care deeply about both our schools and our country and will enthusiastically embrace the opportunity to step up to the plate and get involved when they are called upon to make a difference. So, why are we allowing our education policymakers to usurp our responsibility for our schools? Why are we sitting back and doing nothing about our lack of influence in determining the future of education reform in our nation?

The answer to this pivotal question is deeply rooted in the culture of our democracy. It is baked into the cake of our governing system.

In his book, *Politics For People: Finding a Responsible Public Voice*, David Mathews of the Kettering Foundation writes that "given Americans' sense of civic duty and national pride, how could they have become so disengaged from a political system that is supposedly of the people, by the people, and for the people?" He adds that "we know that people feel pushed out by the system, by a professional political class of lobbyists, politicians, and the media. How could these professional politicians have amassed such power?" (Mathews 1999, 52).

His answer is that our political system functions the way it does because it was designed that way. Our public officials see their role and relationship to the public in the way that the theory of representative government says they should: as guardians of the public interest. They believe the public has an opportunity to vote them out of office if people don't like the job they are doing. Otherwise, they feel they should be left alone to do the job they were elected to do.

Even though most Americans would agree that this is how our representative system of government is supposed to work, it is becoming increasingly clear to many that our system is not working very well today. Here is a prime example of what may be the root cause of the problem.

While many citizens are convinced that our government officials pay no attention to them, many of our elected and unelected officeholders are convinced that they are in constant contact with the public. In addition to letters and telephone calls, they have direct contact with constituents in town hall meetings, discussions at civic clubs, and chance meetings throughout their communities.

Some public officials even believe that they know the public even better than the public knows itself. They also think that citizens have too many other demands on their time at home and the workplace to participate in policy-making. What's more, they believe that most citizens are uninformed and, as a result, it is difficult for them to grasp technical and expert considerations that are central to complex issues.

Earlier in my career, I spent six years working closely with many of our elected officials as a government affairs executive for a Fortune 500 company. I strongly agree with David Mathews who feels that many, perhaps a sizeable majority, of our nation's public officials care about the public even if the public doesn't think so. I also agree with his assessment that many, if not most, of our nation's public officials do not see a real, substantive role for the public.

Changing this viewpoint has been the focus of my work with school superintendents for the past twenty-five years. I know it can be done because I work with superintendents whose boards of education are not usurping their community's responsibility for their schools. They are, instead, involving their citizens in making major educational policy decisions.

References

Mathews, David. 1999. *Politics for People: Finding a Responsible Public Voice.* Urbana, IL: University of Illinois Press.

Part III

Missing from Our National Discussion

Two things are missing from our national discussion about education reform. One is the involvement and voice of reason of the American people—the majority of whom care less about politics and more about doing what is best for our children. The other is the willingness of most school superintendents to step up to the plate and explain how the education reform movement is impacting our schools.

Chapter 12

A Lesson to Be Learned

As you read in chapters 2 and 3, the historical record shows that education reform initiatives have a limited shelf life. Since the 1983 release of *A Nation at Risk*, at least four major reforms—all of which were supported by a wide array of rules and regulations—have been mandated onto the backs of our country's public schools. These reforms include Outcome-Based Education, No Child Left Behind, Race to the Top, and the Common Core Standards.

With that in mind, there is at least a fifty-fifty chance that the Common Core Standards will eventually succumb to the growing pushback against them, fade into the sunset, and eventually be replaced by a new plan from our country's political leaders to "fix our failing schools." The reason why this is likely to occur is simple. Just like previous reforms, the Common Core Standards were imposed on the American people without either their knowledge or input.

To back up what I am saying, all I need to do is refer to the dramatic story of what recently took place in Newark, New Jersey (Russakoff 2014). In essence, it is a story about why a good-faith attempt by the state's two most popular and powerful political leaders to impose an education reform initiative upon Newark's underperforming public schools ultimately failed.

What occurred in Newark serves as an important lesson to be learned about why the voice of the American people needs to be included in our national discussion about education reform. It is a lesson that I have learned over and over again throughout my career. Below are excerpts from this story, which was published in the *New Yorker* magazine.

* * *

Late one night in December, 2009, a black Chevy Tahoe in a caravan of cops and residents moved slowly through some of the most dangerous neighborhoods of Newark. In the back sat the Democratic mayor, Cory Booker, and the Republican governor-elect of New Jersey, Chris Christie. They had become friendly almost a decade earlier, during Christie's years as United States Attorney in Newark, and Booker had invited him to join one of his periodic patrols of the city's busiest drug corridors.

The ostensible purpose of the tour was to show Christie one of Booker's methods of combatting crime. But Booker had another agenda that night. Christie, during his campaign, had made an issue of urban schools. "We're paying caviar prices for failure," he'd said, referring to the billion-dollar annual budget of the Newark public schools, three-quarters of which came from the state. "We have to grab this system by the roots and yank it out and start over. It's outrageous."

Booker had been a champion of vouchers and charter schools for Newark since he was elected to the city council in 1998, and now he wanted to overhaul the school district. He would need Christie's help. The Newark schools had been run by the state since 1995, when a judge ended local control, citing corruption and neglect. A state investigation had concluded, "Evidence shows that the longer children remain in the Newark public schools, the less likely they are to succeed academically." Fifteen years later, the state had its own record of mismanagement, and student achievement had barely budged.

In the back seat of the SUV, Booker proposed that he and Christie work together to transform education in Newark. They later recalled sharing a laugh at the prospect of confounding the political establishment with an alliance between a white suburban Republican and a black urban Democrat. Booker warned that they would face a brutal battle with unions and machine politicians. With seven thousand people on the payroll, the school district was the biggest public employer in a city of roughly two hundred and seventy thousand. As if spoiling for the fight, Christie replied, "Heck, I got maybe six votes in Newark. Why not do the right thing?"

So began one of the nation's most audacious exercises in education reform. The goal was not just to fix the Newark schools but to create a national model for how to turn around an entire school district.

A top-down approach

Early in the summer of 2010, Booker presented Christie with a proposal, stamped "Confidential Draft," titled "Newark Public Schools—A Reform Plan." It called for imposing reform from the top down; a more open political process could be taken captive by unions and machine politicians. "Real change has casualties and those who prospered under the pre-existing order will fight loudly and viciously," the proposal said. Seeking consensus would undercut real reform. One of the goals was to "make

Newark the charter school capital of the nation." The plan called for an "infusion of philanthropic support" to recruit teachers and principals through national school-reform organizations; build sophisticated data and accountability systems; expand charters; and weaken tenure and seniority protections. Philanthropy, unlike government funding, required no public review of priorities or spending. Christie approved the plan, and Booker began pitching it to major donors.

On September 24, 2010, the team described their plan for Newark on *Oprah*. "So, Mr. (Mark) Zuckerberg (billionaire co-founder, chairman and CEO of Facebook)," Oprah asked, "what role are you playing in all of this?" He replied, "I've committed to starting the Startup: Education Foundation, whose first project will be a one-hundred-million-dollar challenge grant." Winfrey interrupted: "One. Hundred. Million. Dollars?" The audience delivered a standing ovation. Three days after Oprah, Booker appeared on MSNBC's *Morning Joe* with Christie and (Secretary of the U.S. Department of Education) Arne Duncan, and vowed, "We have to let Newark lead and not let people drop in from outside and point the way." But Newark wasn't leading . . . In one of the foundation's first expenditures, it paid Tusk Strategies, in New York, $1.3 million to manage the community-engagement campaign. Its centerpiece was ten public forums in which residents were invited to make suggestions to improve the schools. Hundreds of residents came to the first few forums and demanded to be informed and involved. People volunteered to serve as mentors for children who lacked adult support. Shareef Austin, a recreation director at Newark's West Side Park, said, "I have kids every day in my program, their homes are broken by crack. Tears come out of my eyes at night worrying about them. If you haven't been here and grown up through this, you can't help the way we can." Calvin Souder, a lawyer who taught for five years at Barringer High while he was in law school, said that some of his most challenging students were the children of former classmates who had dropped out of school and joined gangs.

Austin said that he and others who volunteered to help were never contacted: "I guess those ideas look little to the people at the top, but they're big to us, because we know what it can mean to the kids."

During the next two years, more than twenty million dollars of Zuckerberg's gift and matching donations went to consulting firms with various specialties: public relations, human resources, communications, data analysis, teacher evaluation . . . The going rate for individual consultants in Newark was a thousand dollars a day. Vivian Cox Fraser, the president of the Urban League of Essex County, observed, "Everybody's getting paid, but Raheem still can't read."

Growing opposition

In February, 2011, the *Star-Ledger* (New Jersey's largest local newspaper) obtained a confidential draft of recommendations by Global Education Advisers that contained a scenario to close or consolidate eleven of the lowest-performing district schools, and to make way for charters and five themed public high schools, to be funded by the Foundation for Newark's Future. The newspaper ran a front-page article listing the schools likely to be affected and disclosed that (Christopher) Cerf, the state commissioner, had founded the consulting firm.

Newark's school advisory board happened to be meeting the night the article was published. The board has no real power, since it's under state control, and meetings were normally sleepy and sparsely attended. Teachers' union leaders had been poised to attack the reform effort, and that evening more than six hundred parents and union activists showed up. One mother shouted, "We not having no wealthy white people coming in here destroying our kids!" From aisles and balconies, people yelled, "Where's Christie!" "Where's Mayor Hollywood!" The main item on the agenda—a report by the Newark schools' facilities director on a hundred and forty million dollars spent in state construction funds, with little to show for it—reinforced people's conviction that someone was making a killing at their children's expense. "Where'd the money go? Where'd the money go?" the crowd chanted.

On a Saturday morning later that month, Booker and Cerf met privately on the Rutgers-Newark campus with twenty civic leaders who had hoped that the Zuckerberg gift would unite the city in the goal of improving the schools. Now they had serious doubts. "It's as if you guys are going out of your way to foment the most opposition possible," Richard Cammarieri, a former school-board member who worked for a community-development organization, told them.

The new superintendent

Cami Anderson emerged as the leading (superintendent) candidate. Thirty-nine years old, she was the daughter of a child-welfare advocate and the community-development director for the Los Angeles mayor Tom Bradley. She had spent her entire career in (school) reform circles.

As for her methods, her friend Rebecca Donner, a novelist, said, "She has her own vision and she won't stop at anything to realize it. If you're faint of heart, if you're easily cowed, if you disagree with her, you're going to feel intimidated." Cerf and Booker came to see that as a virtue. As Cerf put it, "Nobody gets anywhere in this business unless you're willing to get the shit absolutely kicked out of you and keep going. That's Cami."

Christie appointed Anderson in May, 2011 . . . One of her prime initiatives in her first two years was to close and consolidate the twelve lowest-performing kindergarten-through-eighth-grade schools into eight "renew schools." Each was assigned a principal who, borrowing from the charter model, would choose his or her own teaching staff. The schools also got math and literacy coaches and smart boards, along with the new curricula. Teachers worked an extended day and two extra weeks in the summer. Anderson intended to create "proof points" that would show how to turn around failing district schools.

Across the district, in Anderson's first two years, the percentage of students passing the state's standardized tests declined in all but two of the tested grades. She questioned the validity of the tests, saying that they had become harder and the students needier, although she used them to determine which schools were failing and required overhaul. After her first year, she announced a ten-percent gain in the high-school graduation rate, but ACT scores indicated that only two percent of juniors were prepared for college.

Pushback against her plan

Anderson spent much of the fall (of 2013) working with data analysts from the Parthenon Group, an international consulting firm that received roughly three million dollars over two years from Newark philanthropy. She wanted to come up with a plan that would resolve the overlapping complexities of urban schooling . . . She called her plan One Newark.

In the fall, she held dozens of meetings explaining the rationale for One Newark to charter-school leaders, business executives, officials of local foundations, elected officials, clergy, and civic leaders. But participants said she didn't present the specific solutions, because they weren't yet available. Similarly, parents learned in the fall that their schools might be closed or renewed, but they would not get details until December. During the week before the Christmas vacation, Anderson sent her deputies to hastily scheduled school meetings to release the full plan to parents. She anticipated an uproar—"December-palooza," she called it to her staff—which she hoped would diminish by January.

Instead, parents demanded answers and didn't get them. Anderson said that students with learning disabilities would be accommodated at all district schools, but the programs hadn't yet been developed. Families without cars asked how their children would get to better schools across town, since the plan didn't provide transportation. Although Anderson initially announced that charters would take over a number of K–8 schools, it turned out that the charters agreed to serve only K–4; children in grades five through eight would have to go elsewhere . . . The biggest concern was children's safety, particularly in the South Ward, where murders had risen by seventy percent in the past four years.

A community trying to get its schools back

In late January, Randi Weingarten, the president of the American Federation of Teachers, spoke at a school board meeting at First Avenue School in Newark. Five hundred people filled the auditorium; another three hundred and fifty listened in the cafeteria, and more than a hundred stood outside, demanding entry. Weingarten pledged the AFT's support "until this community gets its schools back," and declared, "The nation is watching Newark."

Shavar Jeffries (a member of the school advisory board when Cami Anderson was named superintendent) believes that the Newark backlash could have been avoided. Too often, he said, "education reform … comes across as colonial to people who've been here for decades. It's very missionary, imposed, done to people rather than in cooperation with people."

*   *   *

As I discussed in the previous chapter, our government officials see their role and relationship to the public in the way that the theory of representative government says they should: as guardians of the public interest. They believe the public has an opportunity to vote them out of office if people don't like the job they are doing and that, otherwise, they feel they should be left alone to do the job they were elected to do. What's more, the American people historically have agreed that this is the way our representative government works.

There are times, however, when delegating sole authority and responsibility to our elected officials doesn't work. There are instances where the decisions are so important and impactful that the American people need to be consulted and have an opportunity to help decide what to do or what not to do.

The unilateral decision by Cory Booker and Chris Christie to ignore the school district staff, school parents, and the rest of the community serves as a prime example of one of these instances. By hiring a team of well-paid outside consultants and a superintendent who believed it-is-her-way-or-the-highway to reform the city's public schools, what Booker and Christie basically said to the Newark community was that you don't matter. We are going around you and will do whatever we want to do because you are not that smart and we know better.

This is obviously not the way to get things done if you want to build a trusting and mutually respectful relationship with someone. What they did was insensitive and insulting and ultimately back-fired as a strategy to generate positive and lasting change.

Unfortunately, when it comes to many, if not most, important decisions involving our nation's public schools, a top-down mandated approach like the one taken in Newark is the rule rather than the exception. It is a rare occasion when teachers, parents, and the community are given an opportunity to help make an important decision involving their schools.

Finally, the lesson to be learned from the failed attempt by Cory Booker and Chris Christie to reform Newark's public schools brings to mind a saying that I heard several years ago and have since embraced. It is that you don't mess with people's children or their money without their permission. And, as I have repeatedly learned over the years, you don't mess with their schools without first touching base with them.

References

Russakoff, Dale. 2014, May 19. "Schooled: Cory Booker, Chris Christie, and Mark Zuckerberg Had a Plan to Reform Newark's Schools. They Got an Education," *New Yorker*. http://www.newyorker.com/magazine/2014/05/19/schooled.

Chapter 13

The Voice of the American People

My primary reason for writing this book is to make the case to the America people that our public schools are being overwhelmed by the good intentions of our nation's education policymakers and that in order for citizens to fix the problem they need to get involved in helping shape the future of education reform.

Unfortunately, most people are not aware of what is happening. As a result, the voice of the American people is not being heard and the excessive pressure and stress being placed upon our children and teachers to improve our schools continues to grow.

In this chapter, I explain what I mean when I refer to the voice of the American people. In doing so, I distinguish between the voice of reason of the silent majority of Americans and the loud, confrontational, and what-is-in-it-for-me voice which dominates much of our political discourse today.

First, however, I want to backtrack a little and share a brief story that punctuates the need to make a clear distinction between these two voices.

A friend's concern

In reviewing the manuscript for this book, one of my friends and colleagues brought up a great point regarding the thought of putting the future of our public schools solely into the hands of the American people. Her concern is the squeaky-wheel problem.

She said that as a communications liaison to parents and the community in two school districts and as a school board member in one district, she listened to many parents complain about their local school because "the work is too difficult, there is too much homework, their children should be able to graduate (even though they have a horrible attendance record and have failed one or two classes)" and on and on. Then, when those parents would stand in front of their school board members and demand that the curriculum be "dumbed down," in many instances those school boards would cave in to their demands.

She added that while she thinks parents and other community members should work more closely with their public schools and have greater influence over education policy, she also feels there is a need for national educational goals, standards, and accountability measures. For her, the basic question is: If the state and federal government don't pressure our schools to improve, who will do it?

In addition to making an important and valid point, her question shines a spotlight on a widely accepted belief that lends energy and credibility to the education reform movement. It is the belief that the American people are too busy managing their daily lives and too removed from the realities of today's classroom to get involved in any meaningful way in education reform. And when they do get involved, often it is because they are angry or want something. The logical conclusion to this scenario is that the future of our schools is best served by placing it in the hands of educational experts.

All of this is true—to a point. Most people are busy living their own lives. They are uninformed about what works and what doesn't work in the classroom, and they often get involved with their schools when they have an ax to grind. However, they are in the minority.

The vast majority of Americans are not absorbed by their own needs and concerns. To the contrary, when asked to help deal with a real crisis, they nearly always put their personal agendas aside, step up, and make a difference.

Awakening the silent majority

In working with schools and communities throughout much of my career, I have been blessed to have observed thousands of caring and concerned citizens, many of whom had been sitting on the sidelines unaware of what was happening, successfully tackling serious challenges facing their schools. What has impressed me the most about them is their positive approach in meeting these challenges.

In most instances, they have taken the high road in discussing what often have been divisive topics, such as school tax issues. Instead of ignoring or demeaning the opinions of others who may have disagreed with them, they have been honest, forthright, and respectful. This is in stark contrast to the divisive tone that dominates much of our political discourse today.

Over the past twenty-five years, I have observed dozens of conversations in which citizens with differing opinions were actually listening to one another and valuing one another's feelings and point of view. What's more, many of the people who participated in those conversations had never done anything like this before. They were friends, neighbors, work associates, and relatives who had been asked to attend a coffee discussion or community meeting.

I can't tell how many times I have heard citizens remark at the conclusion of a coffee discussion or community meeting that they had been losing confidence that citizens like themselves could meet like this and have an honest, open, and respectful conversation. They would then add that the past hour and a half had restored their faith in both their community and in one another.

In painting this rosy picture of the American people, I am certainly not implying that these kinds of productive, give-and-take discussions are occurring in most school districts today or even have occurred in every school district in which I have worked. However, they have occurred enough of the time for me to learn that something extraordinarily positive and pure happens when a community is able to escape the hold that politics has on its psyche and tap into the heart and soul of its citizens. It is almost magical.

I have learned and continue to learn that the further away we get from our formal institutions and the network of groups and individuals that support and oppose them politically, the more we are able to tap into the apolitical voice of reason of the American people. So, when I talk about the term *voice of the American people*, I am talking about something quite different from the special interest and ideological voices that dominate the national conversation about our schools in today's politically charged culture.

For me, the true voice of the American people resides within the silent majority of citizens in our country who seldom express their opinions publicly but possess a purity of heart and mind that transcends personal biases and political ideology. The silent majority consists of those Americans who respond when there is a natural disaster or threat to our national security, and, as I have consistently learned over the past twenty-five years, they are the citizens who also respond when given an opportunity to choose between saving money and meeting the educational needs of our children.

The power of love and respect

Although I have seen this uplifting scenario of involvement and support play out many times, two stand out in my mind and serve as vivid examples of how awakening the silent voice of the American people has benefited both our public schools and our communities. Interestingly, both involved strong support from local religious leaders.

Even though they are located in the northeast quadrant of the state of Ohio, the East Canton and Springfield school districts are far apart geographically, and their stories are separated by nearly a decade. What they have in common, however, are the crises they were facing and how their residents were able to tap into the large reservoir of good will, common sense, and love in their communities to overcome their differences and restore trust in both themselves and their schools.

When I arrived in the two school districts, the situations were dire. In each instance, members of the community were at war with one another, teachers and students were demoralized by the lack of public support they were receiving, and school officials had run out of ideas for how to fix the problem.

It would be an understatement to say that the public mood in these districts had degraded to the point of being ugly. In fact, the communities were so divided that some family members were not even speaking to one another. In both districts, the growing anger had gotten out of control and turned into a real mess.

For example, during a community meeting in one of the districts, I remember observing an elderly gentleman break into tears because of his anger, frustration, and disappointment about what was happening to his community. He wasn't alone, however. His feelings were shared by many of his fellow citizens who had not been involved in the early stages of the controversy but were becoming aware of how it was impacting their community and beginning to sense the gravity of the situation.

With the help of religious leaders, the voices of the silent majority of concerned citizens began to turn things around in both communities. And, in doing so, they turned to the healing power of love and respect.

In one of the districts, the priest of the local Catholic church recognized that the anger and frustration that had initially been directed toward the schools was now negatively impacting his community. This realization also occurred in the other district where the community's religious leaders came together and helped lead a healing process of spiritual renewal. In that district, residents lined their streets and driveways with luminaries on the eve of their district's school tax election to signify that they wanted not only to pass the issue but also to move past the months of acrimony and heal their community.

While the voters in both of these Ohio communities approved their school district's tax proposals by wide margins, the healing which led to passage of these tax issues lived well beyond the quiet victory parties that spontaneously occurred after all of the votes were counted. It ushered in new eras of harmony, good will, and trust between school officials and their communities and among the residents themselves.

The magic of dialogue

What drove this healing process? Simply put, it was, in the words of Daniel Yankelovich, the magic of dialogue.

An advisor to corporations, government, and professional organizations, Yankelovich has spent over half a century monitoring change in the American culture and is regarded as the dean of American public opinion research. To help explain how this magic works, I will draw upon the distinction he makes between debate, which describes the tenor and focus of most political conversations, and dialogue (Yankelovich 1999, 39–40).

- When debating, the assumption is that there is a right answer, and we have it. When engaging in dialogue, the assumption is that many people have pieces of the answer and that together we can all craft a solution.
- When debating, we are combative and attempt to prove the other side wrong. When engaging in dialogue, we are col-

laborative and work together toward common understanding.

- When debating, it is about winning. When engaging in dialogue, it is about exploring common ground.
- When debating, we listen to find flaws and make counter-arguments. When engaging in dialogue, we listen to understand and find meaning and agreement.
- When debating, assumptions are defended as truth. When engaging in dialogue, assumptions are revealed for reevaluation.
- When debating, we critique the other side's position. When engaging in dialogue, we reexamine all positions.
- When debating, we defend our own views against the views of others. When engaging in dialogue, we admit that others' thinking can improve on our own thinking.
- When debating, we search for flaws and weaknesses in other positions. When engaging in dialogue, we search for strengths and value in others' positions.
- When debating, we seek a conclusion or vote that ratifies our position. When engaging in dialogue, instead of seeking closure, we discover new options.

The shift from debate to dialogue was largely responsible for the dramatic turnarounds that occurred in the East Canton and Springfield school districts. The silent majority of citizens, who had been sitting on the sidelines watching the growing anger and resentment reach a fever pitch, finally woke up, put their personal biases aside, and engaged in deep and meaningful dialogue. Until then, their voices had been missing from the discussions taking place in the two school districts.

Missing from our national discussion

Unfortunately, that voice of reason has also been missing from our national discussion about education reform. The vast majority of Americans are completely in the dark about how the education reform movement in our country is impacting our schools. As a result, our children and our teachers are suffering, and our tax dollars are being diverted from our schools to a for-profit, privately run education system.

So, why is it missing? While some people believe it is part of an elaborate conspiracy by our political leaders to control our country's education agenda, Daniel Yankelovich has a different explanation:

> The key to successful self-governance in our Age of Information is to create a new balance between (the) public and experts. Today that relationship is badly skewed toward experts at the expense of the public. This out-of-balance condition is not the result of a power struggle (though this is not wholly absent) but a deep-rooted cultural trend that elevates the specialized knowledge of the expert to a place of high honor while denigrating the value of the public's potentially most important contribution—a high level of thoughtful and responsible public judgment. This prejudice is rooted in the dominant Culture of Technical Control (where technical experts control the creation of public policy), which on its positive side has made science, the benefits of modern technology, political freedom, and democracy possible. Yet, even with these impressive accomplishments, a serious difficulty exists. The Cultural of Technical Control saps the national will to confront the obstacles standing in the way of strengthening the quality of public judgment indispensable to self-governance and consensus building. For democracy to flourish, it is not enough to get out the vote. We need better public judgment, and we need to know how to cultivate it (Yankelovich 1991, 11).

I share Yankelovich's view that the erosion of self-governance in our country is rooted in a culture of technical control and not due to an overt power grab by self-serving lawmakers with misguided intentions. Earlier in my career, I worked as a lobbyist for a Fortune 500 company. As a result of that experience, I have a healthy respect for most of our state and federal elected representatives. While there are some exceptions, of course, I found the vast majority of them to be dedicated, well-intentioned public servants trying to do the right thing for our country.

However, like our teachers, our lawmakers today are being bombarded by the growth of government and the increasing responsibilities of their jobs. Overwhelmed by the enormity of the challenges facing our country, they unfortunately have been put into a position where they are forced to rely upon technical experts from the education reform movement and special interest advocacy and opposition groups for much of the information that influences their education policy decisions.

Missing from our national discussion about education reform— and what would be welcomed by many of our elected officials—is the personal involvement, good judgment, and clear voice of reason of the American people who care less about politics and more about doing what is best for our children. It would add a semblance of objectivity and checks and balances that are a rare commodity in our political arena today.

Unfortunately, the playing field on which major policy decisions are being made to reform our schools is uneven. It is dominated by our state and federal government officials who are calling most of the shots without much, if any, meaningful input from the American people. In fact, most Americans are unaware of what is happening.

Everyone working together

Before concluding this chapter, I want to make one final point. And that point needs to be crystal clear.

In stating that the American people need to have a strong voice in determining the future of education reform in our country, I am not suggesting for one minute that they should be the only voice. That would be as detrimental to good decision making as placing it in the hands of a relatively small group of well-intentioned, agenda-driven education reformers.

What I am suggesting—because I have seen it work throughout my career—is that effective, long-term decisions are made when everyone is involved and working together and there is balance in the decision-making process. By saying *everyone*, I include the average person on the street, students, teachers, school administrators, local community leaders, technical experts, our elected and appointed government officials, our corporate leaders, and everyone else I have failed to mention.

Everyone working together is the only way we are going to be able to effectively address the complex issues and concerns facing our nation. And that includes the fate of our country's education system.

References

Yankelovich, Daniel. 1991. *Coming To Public Judgment: Making Democracy Work in a Complex World.* Syracuse, NY: Syracuse University Press.

_____. 1999. *The Magic of Dialogue: Transforming Conflict into Cooperation.* New York: Simon & Schuster.

Chapter 14

Stepping up to the Plate

Back in the so-called "good old days" when I went to school, we were subjected to little, if any, high-stakes testing. The only time I took any high-stakes test was during my junior and senior years when I took the ACT and SAT in preparation for going to college.

In the early 1960s, my classmates and I spent most of our school day sitting quietly in rows listening to our teachers impart information that we would later parrot back to them on a multiple-choice or fill-in-the-blank test. While I had many good and some great teachers, I did not learn high-level thinking skills because they weren't taught in many schools back in those days.

I was fortunate, though. For me, going through grade school, junior high, and high school was a pleasant and rewarding experience. I had parents who motivated me to take school seriously and earn good grades. If fact, they told me that if I didn't make the honor roll, they wouldn't allow me to play sports. That was the clincher.

As a result, I always did well in school. The good old days, however, were not so pleasant and rewarding for many of my classmates.

In my class of eighty-eight students, nearly a third of them suffered through school. Many of my friends fell behind in grade school and felt frustrated and inferior until they either quit school or graduated. Unfortunately for them, there were few if any tests back then to diagnose their learning gaps, and there was a limited range of teaching strategies available to help them catch up educationally.

This is what school was like for millions of America's children prior to 1983 when *A Nation at Risk* announced that America's schools were failing. In this chapter, I will discuss what many school superintendents today acknowledge should have occurred immediately following that wake-up call and why some of them are now stepping up to the plate to rectify the situation.

What should have happened

Two things occurred following *A Nation at Risk*. One is that many of our nation's political leaders grabbed the proverbial bull by the horns and began trying to fix our "failing" schools. What ensued is chronicled in chapters 2 and 3 of this book.

The other thing that occurred is just as significant. Rather than becoming an influential voice in the emerging education reform movement, much of the education community sat back and did nothing. While there were some noted exceptions, most school superintendents and teachers continued to do their jobs as they had previously done them for decades.

When I lay out this scenario and the fact that, in some respects, school superintendents have themselves to blame for the loss of local control of their schools, most of them nod their heads in agreement. Even though they were not superintendents at the time—in fact, some were in grade school—many superintendents now recognize what should have happened after 1983. They realize that their profession should have taken more seriously the wake-up call that America's schools were failing. They acknowledge that it dropped the ball by turning over responsibility for "fixing" our schools to leaders of our nation's education reform movement.

Time to step up to the plate

Today, education reform is being created and controlled by our state and federal government officials, private industrialists, special interest groups, and wealthy philanthropists. There is little, if any, local input or discussion occurring regarding education policy decisions designed to reform our schools.

For the past two years, I have been talking with superintendents throughout our country about the need for them to step up to the plate and let the American people know what is happening to our schools. As you will read in chapter 17, a number of them have already begun this important journey and are providing solid evidence that, stepping up, they can make a positive difference for their schools.

Many other superintendents, however, are discovering that taking that first step is difficult. As one superintendent related to me, "We know what we need to do. We know that we need to utilize our ability to convene the citizens of our communities and engage them in a frank and open discussion about how education reform is impacting their local schools. Something, however, is holding many of us back and it is hard to put a finger on it."

What is holding them back

Having worked with hundreds of school superintendents, I have learned that one of their strongest attributes is, ironically, also holding them back from stepping up and letting the American people know how the education reform movement is impacting their schools. That attribute is the high value that superintendents place on providing positive leadership for their schools and communities.

Their innate desire to provide positive leadership is why most superintendents focus on disseminating good news about their schools and try to refrain from talking about anything negative that might be occurring. However, their desire to accentuate the positive and downplay the negative also creates a false sense of security that everything is fine and obscures major problems that need to be addressed.

One superintendent put it this way: "For decades, our profession has been trapped in a culture in which sharing the good news about our schools is viewed as the way to build public trust and support. The problem is that happy talk puts our citizens to sleep and hides the sense of urgency that motivates them to get involved and take ownership of their public schools."

Another superintendent added: "We desperately want our parents and community to trust us. However, we fail to build authentic trust with them when we only share good news. We need to expose our failures and ask for their help in addressing them."

Today, the premium on disseminating good news is at all-time high for our public schools because they are competing with charter schools for limited state funds. A major concern for local school officials is that placing their school systems in a negative light of any kind could cause parents to withdraw their children and send them to a charter school. Since state funding of our public schools is based upon student enrollment, a school district takes a significant hit financially when it loses just one student to a nonpublic school.

There is another important reason why many superintendents are finding it difficult to step up to the plate and alert the American people about what is happening to our schools. They realize that communicating the full impact of education reform will require more than just sharing a set of positive talking points or publishing an article in the school district newsletter or local newspaper. They understand that what has occurred as a result of the education reform movement is complex and that their citizens will need to be given time to reflect upon how it is impacting them, their schools, and their communities.

As fate would have it, while I was writing this book, the Kettering Foundation released an internal draft report of a research study which provides additional insight into what is holding superintendents back from initiating a conversation in their communities about the impact of the education reform movement on their schools. The Kettering Foundation, an international, non-profit foundation based in Dayton, Ohio, studies what it takes for democracy to work as it should.

According to this forthcoming report (Farkas 2014), one of the most striking observations from this research is the degree to which educational professionals see themselves as working in a climate of relentless criticism and second-guessing. As a result, educators often operate in a defense mode and focus on protecting themselves and their school districts from criticism.

It is no wonder, then, that many superintendents are struggling with the idea of initiating a grassroots community discussion about education reform and exposing themselves and their schools to the potential of receiving more public criticism. However, despite their reluctance to open up "Pandora's box" and risk more second-guessing of them, superintendents are our best hope for arming citizens with the truth about the current state of our nation's public schools.

Why superintendents are our best hope

One of the most serious problems now facing our country is that the vast majority of Americans no longer trust most of our major institutions—including our government. For example, the percentage of citizens who trust the US Congress slipped to an all-time low of 9 percent in November of 2013 and, as the graph on the following page shows (McCarthy 2014), has not reached 15 percent since then.

Do you approve or disapprove of the way Congress is handling its job?

■ % Approve

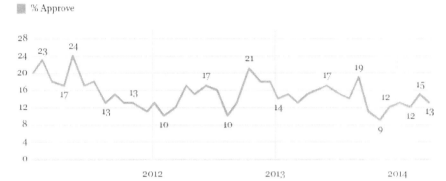

Trend since January 2011; for earlier trends, see Gallup.com

GALLUP

Fortunately, the American people still have faith in their local public schools. In the "45th Annual PDK/Gallup Poll of the Public's Attitudes Toward the Public Schools," citizens reported that they are highly satisfied with their local schools. More than 70 percent have trust and confidence in their teachers and 53 percent gave their schools an A or B, the highest rating ever recorded in the poll (PDK/Gallup 2013).

Having worked with superintendents throughout my career, the public's faith in their local schools is nearly always justified. I can state without hesitation that most superintendents are honest, dependable, and caring individuals. Even more importantly, they have the best interest of their students and communities in mind.

If I want to know the truth about anything related to our public schools, I immediately turn to my superintendent friends and colleagues. I trust them implicitly.

Most superintendents are objective and see the big picture. They know how our schools are really doing, and they are ideally positioned to help lead a frank and open national grassroots discussion about the future of education reform.

In chapter 19, I lay out specific steps that we can take as individual citizens to help initiate this vitally important and long-overdue discussion.

References

Farkas, Steve. 2014. "Maze of Mistrust: How District Politics and Crosstalk Are Stalling Efforts to Improve Public Education." A forthcoming report of a research study conducted by the Kettering Foundation and FDR Group. Kettering.org.

McCarthy, Justin. 2014, April 10. "No Improvement for Congress' Job Approval Rating." *Gallup Politics*. http://www.gallup.com/poll/168428/no-improvement-congressional-approval.aspx.

PDK/Gallup. 2013. "45th Annual Phi Delta Kappan/Gallup Poll of the Public's Attitudes Toward the Public Schools." *Kappan*.

Part IV

Reason for Hope

Whether it has involved responding to a natural disaster, a threat to our national security, or the educational needs of our children, the American people have always come through when they clearly understand why they are needed. When they realize that our public schools are at a turning point, they will rise to the occasion once again.

Chapter 15

My Turning Point

In 1996, I had a life-changing experience while working in a rural school district in northeast Ohio. That experience became the major turning point in my career and continues to be my standard for how the American people need to be treated.

The following account of what occurred was written by the school district's superintendent of schools for my book, *The Power of Public Engagement: A Beacon of Hope for America's Schools* (Werstler 1999, 183–191).

* * *

HOLMES COUNTY, Ohio—In Holmes County, things are a little different from how they are in most other places. The first tip-off of this is the number of horse-drawn buggies and wagons that travel along the roadways. In fact, road signs warning drivers of horseless carriages to watch out for these slower-moving vehicles are placed in strategic locations throughout the county.

Home to the world's highest concentration of Amish residents, Holmes County has a pace of life that is slower than it is elsewhere. People don't seem to be in as much of a hurry as folks in other communities. There is a feeling of serenity here that eludes much of the rest of the civilized world.

Nestled among the quiet farms that dominate the county's landscape is the West Holmes School District. A large district geographically, West Holmes covers 250 square miles and enrolls 2,680 students.

So how did it happen that one of the most dramatic examples of the power of public engagement comes from this part of Ohio? Well, it all started one day when our building principals and I began talking informally about a serious problem that had been plaguing the district for at least ten years. The problem was class sizes. They were simply too large.

Slow at first

At first, our conversation focused on all the reasons local residents were not in the mood to tackle this problem. We reminded ourselves of how a proposed bond issue to build a new junior high building had been soundly defeated a few years before. We also talked about how expensive it would be to add the space and hire the additional teachers we really needed in order to reduce our increasing class sizes. Besides, we had bought hook, line, and sinker into the idea that what the public wanted, more than anything else, was for us to be efficient and to do more with less.

It took four meetings before we began to let go of the be-efficient-at-all costs way of thinking which controlled our perspective. It was only after we drew some of our most highly respected teachers into our discussion that we began to realize that we had no choice. If we were going to be educational leaders and do what was best for children, we had to be brutally honest with both ourselves and our residents and expose the classroom conditions that really existed.

It was not easy—at least at first. We had grown comfortable with "making do" and proudly saying to the world that "whatever you give us, we'll make it work." Now, we had to tell the whole truth. We had to let everyone know that the children in our school district were being shortchanged. We had to share enrollment projections which showed that the overcrowding was going to slowly increase and that the problems associated with it were going to gradually grow worse.

The teachers knew

It was probably the teachers who gave us the courage to say what had to be said. When we asked our teachers how important class size was, there was no hesitation. As one kindergarten teacher clearly put it, "When a child finishes kindergarten, that child decides whether or not he or she likes school. If we lose them then because our class sizes are too large, we lose them forever." Nearly all of the West Holmes teachers, including the high school staff, agreed that student success is determined early in school, usually by the third or fourth grade.

The internal discussion with our building principals and some of their key teachers about the impact of increasing student enrollment and the importance of class size took several weeks. However, we finally came to the conclusion that, yes, class size does make a difference and that in the primary grades it needs to be between twenty and twenty-two students, and in the higher grades it needs to be, at most, twenty-five. Up to that point, the class size standard we were willing to accept was thirty children in a classroom.

One of our second grade teachers said what the rest of our elementary staff knew only too well: "When I have thirty children in my classroom, I lose six or eight of them. No matter how hard I try, I don't have enough time to give them the attention they need. These are the children who are falling through the cracks in our schools, and it is a big, big problem. I can't begin to tell you how frustrating it is to know that you could make a much bigger difference for these children if you had smaller class sizes."

Class sizes too large

At this point, the stage was set to expand our discussion, and we did. About two months after our first meeting with building principals, we invited a key teacher from each building, the leaders of the teachers' association, and our principals to a breakfast meeting on the second floor of the Holmes County Human Services building.

After presenting a graphic picture of the growing student enrollment facing the district, I stopped a minute and let the impact of the information sink in. You could see the gloom and doom on the faces of many of the sixteen people in attendance that morning.

Then, I said, "This is tough for me to say, but it has to be said. Class sizes in this school district are too large." Well, the silence was deafening. You could have heard a pin drop.

After what seemed like an eternity, one by one, the teachers began to open up and share heartfelt words that many had kept bottled up for a number of years. Every teacher in the room that day said, "Yes, we agree that our class sizes are much too large, and we have known it for a long time. Is it now safe for us to say it out loud?"

The turning point

This served as a turning point in our effort to be brutally honest with the residents of the West Holmes School District. Rather than be limited by the assumption that communicating with citizens meant trying to make them feel good about the schools by sharing only positive information with them, we now had the chance to say what it was really like in the West Holmes Schools. We could now say that while we have a good school system with teachers who are doing the best they can, students are falling through the cracks because our class sizes are too big.

Following this important meeting, the teachers went back to

their buildings and began to talk with their peers. They also began to spread the word among their friends and neighbors.

A few weeks later at the conclusion of one of our board of education meetings, we brought the board into the middle of the discussion. While the board members were aware of what we were doing, they were still of the mind that "since it has seemingly worked for the last twenty years, it is okay to continue to make do."

Each building principal and one or two teachers from each building shared their feelings in an open and heartfelt way. It was an emotional time for everyone. The school board was finally having an opportunity to see and feel firsthand the impact of years and years of program cuts.

After the principals and teachers said what they had to say, it was clear to the school board that something had to be done about the class size problem. That night, the line in the sand was drawn. The popular idea that the public schools "should be doing more with less" at any cost was toppled, and the focus returned to the children.

Parent meeting

The goal now was to search for the delicate balance between being efficient and providing a quality education. To help find this balance, the principals invited ten to fifteen parents from their buildings to attend a special briefing to talk about the situation. Eighty parents showed up. Just before the meeting began, one of the parents said, "Yeah, you guys just got us here to tell us you want more money." The response to him was emphatic, "No, we are not going to do that. We are going to share some information with you and ask for your advice."

After the building principals and teachers told their stories, the parents divided into six groups to talk about what they had just heard. We asked them to tell us what they thought about class size and whether it was important. Within the first five minutes, they had already agreed that class size is one of the key ingredients to providing the support that students need today and that it is a serious problem at West Holmes. The rest of the discussion focused upon potential solutions.

Following brief summations by each group of parents, it was clear that two avenues were available to fix the class size problem. One was to build more classrooms and the other was to double up on the use of existing classroom space. The dilemma of this alternative use of existing facilities strategy was that adding more space would be expensive and reusing existing space would be inconvenient and, to some degree, compromise educational quality.

However, both approaches were far superior to cramming thirty children into elementary classrooms and severely limiting course offerings for middle school and high school students. When this group of parents reconvened a couple of weeks later, they split into two committees. One committee began to look for the best way to add more classrooms, while the other group started to explore the advantages and disadvantages of year-round school and split sessions as solutions to the class-size problem.

Citizen-driven discussions

It is important to point out that these discussions were citizen-driven. While school board members and the administrative team were part of the early conversations, they did not take any official positions as a board of education. If they had, it would have ended public discussion. The opportunity and responsibility for lowering class sizes then would have shifted from the community and ended up back in the laps of school officials.

After many meetings and weeks of exploration and study, the recommendation from the building committee was to construct a new high school, add ten classrooms to the four other buildings in the district, and turn the existing high school into a middle school housing grades six, seven, and eight.

The recommended alternative, to be implemented if a bond issue for additional classroom space were rejected, was split sessions for middle school and high school students. After the two groups of parents met for a third time and shared their recommendations, the stage was set to reach further into the community and bring more citizens into the discussion.

After more than a year of serious dialogue among parents, school board members, teachers, administrators, and other school employees, the conversation was expanded further to include the rest of the community.

Again, no decisions had yet been made by the school board. All options were still open to change.

On May 20, the board hosted a State of the Schools community meeting. Letters were mailed to every school district resident, and phone calls were made to hundreds of parents and civic and neighborhood leaders. At the meeting attended by four hundred citizens, we presented an unedited version of the complete picture.

The first paragraph of the introduction to the State of the Schools background information booklet set the tone for the meeting: "The purpose of this meeting tonight is to discuss the class size and instructional space needs of the school district. We know that we have a growing student population, and we need solutions on how to deal with it. Class size affects the quality of our educational programs. We will share with you our observations on that important issue. Although we are still gathering input before a final decision is made, we are at a point where we need a solution. Your input this evening will be very valuable and important."

The parent committees also presented their recommendations regarding the long-term and short-term solutions to the class size problem, and a panel of teachers spoke from the heart about why the problem had reached a crisis point and needed to be resolved.

The class size issue, in fact, had become so important to parents that the alternative solution committee wanted to implement split sessions immediately. They didn't want to wait until November when voters were going to be given the opportunity to approve a bond issue to build additional classrooms. Fortunately, we were able to convince them that we needed to wait and let the voters make the decision about what to do about our overcrowding problem.

During the summer, we focused our attention on talking with people who had not yet become part of the community-wide dialogue. About thirty of us identified ten people each whom we knew, and we met one-on-one with them.

The impact of having quality discussions with another 300 school district residents was powerful. Most of them had never been approached this way before. They had never been asked for their advice while they still had a chance to have an impact. To give as many people as possible the opportunity to become part of the final decision, the school board held off placing the bond issue on the ballot until the filing deadline in late August.

Birdie's Restaurant

One of the conversations that took place that summer involved a small group of long-time community residents and me. Every morning, eight to ten of them meet at Birdie's Restaurant. Every small town has a place like this where a lot of "old timers" seem to hang out. Nobody stays the whole time. They just float in and out.

Well, one day, one of the regulars in this close-knit group who had also served on the new building committee, suggested that I drop in sometime and talk with everyone about the class size problem. So one morning, I rambled in, sat down, and ordered a cup of coffee.

In a group like this, you wait until it is your turn to talk, and you know when it is your turn because they let you know—which usually is after everybody has said what they have to say two or three times. When it finally got around to the topic of the schools,

I just happened to have a stack of handouts that we had distributed at the State of the Schools meeting.

As soon as I began to go through the handout, they started asking this question and that question. Then, someone said, "Yeah, we do have a good school system here, and we need to take care of those kids, and class sizes at the elementary level are really getting big. How much do you say you can do this for?" I said about $18 million, and they responded, "That's not too bad."

When I look back at what made the difference in the West Holmes School District during that year-and-a-half period, it is pretty simple. After lengthy conversations, the board of education, the school administration, teachers, school support staff, and a core group of concerned parents drew a line in the sand and said, "We cannot continue this way any longer. The way it is now is harmful for our kids. Because of our large class sizes, our teachers are not able to do the job they know how to do. We can't tolerate this anymore."

When people feel responsible

Once the line had been drawn in the sand, the community not only began to feel a sense of responsibility to do something about it, but residents led the effort to get a bond issue placed on the ballot.

It had reached the point where it was out of the hands of the school board. The community was demanding that the class-size problem be fixed. Even a small but important group of local business leaders, who generally feel that the schools need to follow the lead of business and learn how to do more with less, jumped on the bandwagon after they were asked to work with the architect to fine-tune the details of the proposed high school and to find some land on which to put it.

Once provided with the opportunity to help make a difference, the response of these business leaders was, "Let's go out and get it done."

By the time school started in late August, it was clear to many residents why a bond issue was going to be on the ballot. It was also clear that the option for reducing class sizes was implementing split sessions.

In September, the groundwork was laid for the bond issue campaign. Virtually hundreds of seeds of understanding about why a bond issue was needed had been sown throughout the school district. Many residents from all walks of life felt a sense of urgency that something needed to be done about the class-size problem.

As more and more people began to focus their attention on the upcoming bond issue election, these seeds of understanding started to germinate. Citizens who had helped create the options for resolving the class-size problem and, as a result, clearly understood why the money was needed, became sounding boards for others who were just beginning to join the community discussion.

Finally, the tenor of the dialogue became so intense that the community grapevine began to spread the word to all school district residents about what was really at stake for the school children at West Holmes.

On November 5, 1996, voters approved the bond issue by a 58-to-42-percent margin.

References

Werstler, Dean P. 1999. "Class Size: The Core Concern." In *The Power of Public Engagement: A Beacon of Hope for America's Schools*. Manhattan, KS: The MASTER Teacher, Inc.

Chapter 16

Alive and Well

In my introduction to this book, I asked you to think about how we as a nation responded to the attack on Pearl Harbor, the leveling of the Twin Towers, the hurricane that plummeted the New Jersey coast, and the tornado that devastated Joplin, Missouri.

Then, I continued by stating that we did what we always do when faced with a natural disaster or a threat to our national security. We came together, opened our wallets, rolled up our sleeves, and fixed the problem.

Stepping up to the plate and making a difference when needed is a deeply ingrained value in our nation's culture, and it is not limited to big, life-changing events. In our communities, we are making a difference every day in less dramatic but important ways. Having worked in more than three hundred public school districts over the past twenty-five years, I have seen firsthand how citizens nearly always respond to the educational needs of our children when they are asked to help.

Throughout my career—and to this day—I have seen over and over again that the American spirit is alive and well. Despite national opinion polls showing that many people are worried about the future of our country, they continue to step up when they are needed and make a difference—just as they did eighteen years ago in the West Holmes School District.

For the remainder of this chapter, I provide more evidence of the power of the American spirit. For this evidence, I draw upon my work with our public schools and the Kettering Foundation.

*　*　*

Why the portrait of Jesus had to be removed

The resiliency of the American spirit was put to the test in 1993 for a suburban community twenty miles south of Cleveland, Ohio. A firsthand account of what occurred in the Medina City School District is provided by Charles Irish who was serving as the district's superintendent of schools.

Since 1946, a portrait of Jesus had hung in Garfield Elementary in honor of a beloved school superintendent who had passed away. However, everything changed when a community member demanded that the portrait be removed.

In short order, we had drawn coast-to-coast attention and became the battle ground for civil rights and religious groups. Individual letters and newspaper editorials poured in from all corners of the nation, demanding this and threatening that. Even my board of education was split. Something had to give.

I thought I would resolve the issue quickly by convening a large group of the local clergy, all of whom were from Christian denominations. After all, Medina is a "Christian" community and, besides, there really wasn't a choice about the final outcome. The portrait had to be removed. Our role would be to come together and figure out how to make that happen as painlessly and as respectfully as possible.

However, I was wrong. This group was divided. In observing their facial expressions and other aspects of their body language, including even their choice of seating on which side of the room, I could clearly see that this wasn't going to be easy.

A plea for civility

Before the meeting began, some of them let it be known to everyone in the room that there would be a severe price to pay if the picture were removed. It was obvious that they were upset about the situation, and they were not in the mood for discussing alternative points of view. Still, we tried to talk. During an unfruitful exchange between some of the participants, a Methodist minister, who had remained silent to this point, spoke forcefully, pleading for a civil and thoughtful discussion.

The clock was ticking on the timeline established by the American Civil Liberties Union before it would bring suit against the school district. Therefore, at our next public meeting, I found it necessary to make a statement about the school district's next steps. The audience was large and diverse. Several major Ohio TV and newspaper reporters also were in attendance.

While many local citizens were there to express their desire to resolve this issue without being drawn into a highly publicized lawsuit, some individuals who had been spurred by groups and organizations outside our community were at the meeting itching for a fight.

The time came for me to make my statement. It was short. I simply said, "We're not going to do anything just yet until we've had time to talk about this as a community. It is our community, and it is our decision. We'll let you know what we decide when we decide." Although these comments may have sounded bold at the time, they were nothing more than an attempt to get off the stage and to buy time to figure out how we were going to have a productive community conversation in the midst of so much anger.

We began our effort by organizing meetings in all of the usual places: churches, civic halls, even in some individuals' homes. Our role was simple. We were there to listen.

Most of the gatherings brought together people of a like mind, and the participants were not shy about expressing their opinions about how they felt about opposing viewpoints. It soon became apparent to us that the most negatively vocal meetings were those led by someone from our school district leadership team. People on both sides of the issue often attended and freely expressed anger. And we were the recipients of it.

Several of the get-togethers were arranged by the Methodist minister who had called for the community members to be civil with one another as they held their discussions. I attended a couple of his meetings that brought together individuals with differing perspectives. I found them to be enlightening.

While meeting attendees passionately expressed their convictions, the conversations were surprisingly civil. I didn't perceive that anyone had a change of heart, but I sensed that they did listen to one another.

Putting things into perspective

The day before the inescapable board of education meeting where a decision about the portrait was to be made, I came upon a small group talking in a local restaurant. Members of the group had organized the meeting themselves, and, when they saw me, they invited me to join them.

Even though they had different perspectives, they were all troubled with the situation. Then, one woman made a comment to the group that resonated with what many citizens in our community were feeling. She said: "I know that it isn't right to have that picture hanging there, but I just feel like we're losing." She had just summed up for me the entire controversy in one sentence.

I talked with her later and asked her what she meant by her statement. She told me that she initially came to the issue believing that the picture needed to stay. However, in the interim she had several conversations with friends and fellow church members. Apparently the conversations took many turns, but, in time, she formed her opinion that the picture should be removed. Still, it left her with a deep sadness: "I just feel like we're losing."

The next evening I used her words to express what I had learned from the community as I announced that the picture would be moved to the Methodist church across the street where the honored superintendent had been a member. Replacing it would be a plaque reading, "A portrait of Jesus hung in this location from 1946 until it was removed in 1993 because of 2nd Amendment concerns."

While few residents had changed their minds about what to do with the portrait of Jesus, the eventual "ceremony" around the transfer of the portrait enabled them to accept the reality that the portrait of Jesus had to be removed.

In the tradition of what we as a nation do when faced with a crisis, the residents of the Medina City School District stepped up to the task of fixing a difficult problem and proved once again that the American spirit is alive and well.

*   *   *

A frank and open community conversation

In the spring of 2005, I received a phone call from Bob Scott, the superintendent of a suburban school district enrolling 3,500 students west of Cleveland. The purpose of his call was to ask if I would be interested in working with his community to pass a school tax issue that had recently been defeated by a two-to-one margin. I told him I would if he and his campaign leadership team would be willing to challenge the conventional wisdom about how to build public support for his district's proposed tax increase. In the following paragraphs, Bob shares his story about the vitality and resilience of the American spirit in his community.

In August of 2005, the Avon Lake City School District Board of Education, two dozen school supporters, and I decided to challenge the conventional wisdom about how to pass a school tax issue.

Instead of forming a citizens' committee to organize and wage a traditional in-your-face, vote-yes advocacy campaign, we created a partnership of citizens representing different voices in our school district to lead a frank and open community conversation. Most importantly, the conversation would not be just about the upcoming tax proposal but also about other issues and concerns impacting our schools and community.

Our goal was not to just talk but also to listen. Information was provided about the district and the proposed tax levy, but there was no script, and there was no sales pitch. Regardless of the setting, the focus was on two-way communication. Our ultimate objective was to strengthen the bond of trust between our schools and community.

An entirely different approach

On the surface, the communication strategies that were utilized looked a lot like traditional levy campaign strategies. Fifty informal coffee discussions were held. Two hundred volunteers distributed information to every household in the community. And school board members spoke with one hundred forty key neighborhood leaders and hosted two district-wide meetings. However, a look beneath the surface reveals an entirely different approach to campaigning.

Unlike the typical levy campaign, in which the appeal is made to the "Yes" voters and the message is about separating the "good guys" (school supporters) from the "bad guys" (school nonsupporters), this time, the audience and the message were different. The audience shifted dramatically to include those who had been opposed to the previous levy.

In the multitude of community conversations that occurred during those three months, we worked hard to include as many citizens as possible—especially those who historically had not been supportive of school tax issues. Our theme, "Join the Community Conversation," was created to attract all of the voices in our school district. Two months prior to the levy election, yard signs bearing this theme and two companion signs reading "Want to know more?" and "Call 933-0202" were placed in a Burma-shave-sign fashion at strategic locations throughout our community.

Simultaneously, the Avon Lake Board of Education mailed a letter and postage-paid reply card to all school district residents inviting them to join in this important community conversation. More than one hundred cards were returned from residents expressing an interest in becoming involved in coffee discussions with school board members.

To remain true to our commitment to lead a frank and open discussion about more than just the proposed operating levy, neither the school board nor the community partnership team attempted to convince residents to vote "Yes" for the proposed tax increase. There were no "Vote Yes for the Levy" signs, no promotional flyers asking residents to support the levy, and no newspaper ads, radio commercials, or TV spots asking them to vote "Yes."

This strategy was unsettling for many of the district's most enthusiastic school supporters, old levy pros, and diehard political campaigners. In the past, these traditional campaign symbols had provided them with a sense of security. Now these symbols were nowhere in sight.

For three months, school district residents were saturated with opportunities to "Join the Community Conversation" about their schools. And for three months, the leaders of this grassroots community conversation resisted the temptation to revert back to in-your-face levy advocacy tactics that are utilized in many school tax campaigns.

Building understanding and trust

The positive impact of employing this community conversation strategy to discuss the provisions of our proposed operating levy became evident in two significant ways. First, a growing number of citizens began to understand and trust that the tax increase was really needed. As a result, even though the levy was defeated, the margin of defeat was reduced to 6 percent—down from the 30 percent deficit six months earlier.

Secondly, the residue of anger and frustration that usually accompanies a school tax election did not materialize. Rather than dividing our community into pro-levy and anti-levy camps and polarizing our district with a divisive campaign, the tone established by holding a district-wide community conversation helped us eliminate organized resistance to the levy and move forward in a positive way after the election.

Nine days after the November election, with a wind chill factor dipping into the teens, fifty influential leaders from our community showed up at the Avon Lake Library to discuss how to continue our community conversation. As a result of this discussion, we scheduled a "State of the Schools" meeting for all of our school district's residents.

Two months later, with more than one hundred people in attendance at this district-wide community meeting, the Avon Lake Board of Education opened with a discussion about the impact of the November levy defeat and then asked the attendees whether they felt the next step should be to make additional budget reductions or place the operating levy back on the ballot. The overwhelming response was to immediately place it on the May ballot.

On May 2, the operating levy was overwhelmingly approved by 63 percent of the voters.

In working with school officials and residents in the Avon Lake School District, I learned a lot more than just how to more effectively pass a school tax issue. I learned that what had occurred in the West Holmes and Medina school districts was not a fluke. In Avon Lake, I discovered once again that the American spirit is alive and well. Just as they have done throughout our nation's history, our citizens will rise to the occasion when they are needed and successfully meet an important challenge.

*   *   *

Thank you for all you do

Deer Park is a close-knit community nestled along the city limits of Cincinnati, Ohio, and Jeff Langdon was its newly appointed superintendent of schools. His story serves as another example of how much the American people care and will come together and do whatever it takes to fix an urgent problem.

When Jeff Langdon was named superintendent of the Deer Park Community City School District, the school system was facing a number of important challenges that needed to be addressed. In early January of 2013, he initiated a year-long discussion with school district residents.

Between January and the end of school in early June, Jeff attended thirty coffee discussions with more than four hundred school district residents. During these frank and open conversations, residents discussed a wide range of topics, which included school district finances, the Common Core Standards, and the question of whether and/or when to place a school tax issue on the ballot in order to avoid having to reduce educational services.

The overwhelming recommendation from these coffee conversations was to place an operating levy on the November 2013 ballot. However, unlike what occurs in many other school districts when a tax issue is placed on the ballot, the frank and open conversation continued.

Rather than insulting residents by telling them how to vote and spend their money, the citizens' committee supporting the tax levy reached out to the community and thanked residents for everything they were already doing to support the Deer Park Schools. There was not one campaign sign asking or telling residents to vote for the levy.

Dignity and respect

Instead, a thousand signs with the message, "Thank you for all that you do for our Deer Park Schools," appeared throughout the district. The goal of this "thank you" initiative was to give voters the dignity and respect they deserve and to generate conversations with them.

During September and October, fifty volunteers wearing "Thank you for all that you do for our Deer Park Schools" T-shirts each contacted twenty households, thanked residents for their support of the Deer Park Schools and, whenever possible, engaged in conversations about the operating levy and other concerns. This is what campaign volunteers said when a community member greeted them at the door:

Hello. My name is _____. I am a (teacher, parent, community member, etc.) in the Deer Park School District and I would like to talk with you about our school system. Is this a good time? (If no, the campaign volunteer asked when would be a better time to talk. If yes, the volunteer thanked the person for his or her time and continued …)

First of all, on behalf of our teachers, our parents, and our community, I want to personally thank you for your financial support of our schools. If it weren't for your support over the years, the Deer Park Schools wouldn't be the quality school system that it is today.

Secondly, I want to let you know that I am not here to tell you how to vote or spend your money. That is none of my business. I would, however, like to talk with you about the $7.9 million continuing operating levy for our schools that will be voted on November 5 and answer or get you the answer to any questions or concerns you may have regarding this levy or our schools in general. (The volunteer gave the person a few seconds to collect his or her thoughts and before responding to the volunteer's opening remarks. The goal was to engage the community member in a frank and open conversation and it didn't matter if it was for a couple of minutes or for half an hour or more.)

(At the conclusion of each conversation, the campaign volunteer handed the person a levy brochure and said . . .) Thank you, once again, for your time. I hope that the information in this brochure and the information on the levy website which is referenced in the brochure are helpful.

The response from residents was heartwarming. By being approached in such a respectful way, many of them opened up and engaged in meaningful conversations with the levy volunteers which included the superintendent, other school administrators, and teachers.

On November 5, residents let Jeff know what they thought of the approach of engaging them in the decision to place an operating levy on the ballot and of the thank-you campaign that followed. They passed it on the first attempt by an overwhelming margin of 62 to 38 percent.

What I learned

Much of what I learned working in the Deer Park School District reinforces what I have been learning over the past twenty-five years. And it is that, although most people may be disconnected to what is happening in their schools, they are neither uncaring nor stupid.

People know when they are being patronized, demeaned, or

misled. They know, for example, when their school leaders cross the line and intrude in their personal space by telling them how to vote and spend their money.

The lesson from Deer Park is that showing the American people a little dignity and respect goes a long way. It renews their faith—at least temporarily—in one major US institution: their public schools.

* * *

Bertha Gilkey

Examples of how the American spirit is alive and well are not limited to the public schools and the communities they serve. Kettering Foundation President David Mathews includes in his book, Politics for People *(Mathews 1999, 138–39) a story about one person named Bertha Gilkey who embodies this spirit.*

Bertha Gilkey is the leader of a tenants' project in St. Louis and lives in Cochran Gardens, a public housing project which today is noted for flower-lined paths, clean buildings, play equipment, and social cohesion. She lived in this very same housing project when it was filled with drugs, crime, prostitution, garbage and urine in the halls, broken windows, and graffiti.

While the Gardens may not still be perfect, the changes she helped make were dramatic and profound. Improvements began with a simple but powerful first step.

At the outset, one of the major problems in the project was vandalism of the laundry room. When the machines were destroyed, the tenants demanded that the project's management install new ones. Even when pressured by rent strikes, the management was increasingly resistant to throw good money after bad.

Then one day, the tenants added a new tactic to their strategy. This strategy set in motion a transformation of the Gardens.

The first goal for Bertha Gilkey and her neighbors was to

have a locked and painted door for the laundry. The tenants raised funds in the project to buy a lock and a few cans of paint. It wasn't much, but it demonstrated that the tenants could do something on their own. Next came a campaign to get everyone to paint their hallways.

On the heels of these small but encouraging achievements, the tenants then approached the building management. This time they came with more than needs and demands. They came with capacities and even accomplishments. They had something to offer.

In time, the often-troubled tenant-management relationship changed for the better. As the tenants took responsibility for themselves, they ceased to be wards of the manager. Tenants became the planners rather than the planned for. They became citizens of their neighborhood.

The story of Bertha Gilkey demonstrates once again that when citizens claim responsibility, whether it is for their local public housing project or their schools, they develop a sense that they are the solution rather than bystanders or victims. By holding themselves responsible, they rediscover their ability to step up to the plate and make a difference.

* * *

These stories chronicling the power and viability of the American spirit are not unique. Even as I write this book, there are several developing scenarios like these that I could share.

As I stated at the beginning of this chapter, stepping up to the plate and making a difference when needed is a deeply ingrained value in our nation's culture, and it is not limited to big, life-changing events. In our communities, we are making a difference every day in less dramatic but important ways.

Throughout my career, I have seen firsthand how citizens will nearly always respond to the educational needs of our children when they are asked to help. Today, our schoolchildren need our help.

In the next chapter, I provide encouraging evidence that the stage is set for the American people to address the problems being generated by the current education reform movement and help shape the future of our nation's public schools.

References

Mathews, David. 1999. *Politics for People: Finding a Responsible Public Voice.* Urbana, IL: University of Illinois Press.

Chapter 17

The Stage Is Set

Four major societal trends have set the stage for the American people to get involved in helping shape the future of our schools. These trends include the loss of confidence in our political leaders, growing concern about the growth of government, latent opposition to the education reform agenda, and our innate need to make a difference.

I believe that the synergy being created by these trends is moving our nation toward a tipping point in which the American people will say enough is enough, and step up to help shape the future of our schools.

Loss of confidence in our political leaders

In chapter 14, I pointed out that the percentage of citizens who trust the US Congress slipped to an all-time low of 9 percent in November of 2013 and has not reached 15 percent since then (McCarthy April 2014). Based upon a Gallup poll conducted in June of 2014, Americans' confidence in all three branches of the US government had fallen, reaching record lows for the Supreme Court at 30 percent and Congress at 7 percent, and a six-year low for the presidency at 29 percent (McCarthy June 2014).

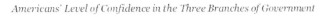

Americans' Level of Confidence in the Three Branches of Government
% Great deal/Quite a lot

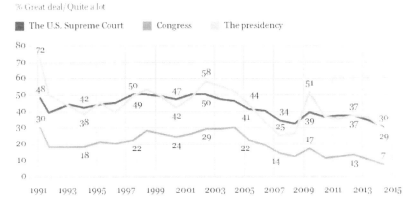

Growing concern about the growth of government

In addition to the erosion of confidence in our political leaders, the American people are deeply concerned about the increasing overreach of our federal government. In a national opinion survey conducted in December of 2013, Gallup reported that 72 percent of Americans say big government is a greater threat to the United States in the future than is big business or big labor, a record high in the nearly fifty-year history of this question. The prior high for big government was 65 percent in 1999 and 2000 (Jones 2013).

Views of Biggest Threat to U.S. in Future
In your opinion, which of the following will be the biggest threat to the country in the future -- big business, big labor, or big government?

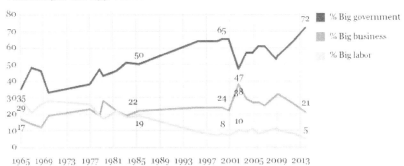

Latent opposition to the education reform agenda

When it comes to education reform in our country, the Common Core Standards are currently in the eye of the storm. While most of the opposition to these standards has been limited to conservative radio talk show hosts, members of Tea Party groups, school parents, and some educators, opposition to the Common Core Standards is likely to grow as the American people begin to learn how the education reform movement is impacting them and their schools.

In their introduction to the 2013 annual survey report of the public's attitudes toward the public schools conducted by Phi Delta Kappan and the Gallup polling organization, the authors of the report state that "until the fall 2012, the Common Core enjoyed widespread acceptance. It was even touted in a national advertising campaign by ExxonMobil Corp. But opposition gathered, starting with scattered protests by conservatives at state capitals who renounced the standards as a federal government overreach. Next, the Republican National Committee in April 2013 unexpectedly adopted a resolution rejecting implementation of the Common Core. The battle continues" (PDK/Gallup 2013, 9).

Highlights of the 2013 PDK/Gallup report indicate that the vast majority of Americans were unaware of the Common Core Standards. However, when they were made aware of them, they opposed many of the provisions of both the Common Core and other educational standards being mandated by the education reform movement. Here is some of the evidence that this is true:

- In 2013, only slightly more than one third of all Americans and fewer than half of those with children in the public schools recognized the Common Core Standards.

- Among the third who have heard of the Common Core

Standards, only four of ten think these standards can help make education in the United States more competitive globally. A majority of Americans said the standards will make the United States less competitive or have no effect.

- Fewer than one of four Americans said the increase in student testing has helped improve local public schools.

- Fifty-eight percent oppose requiring that teacher evaluations include student scores on standardized tests.

- Almost two of three Americans oppose releasing information to newspapers about how students of individual teachers perform on standardized tests.

- When the American people were asked if they favor or oppose allowing students and parents to choose a private school to attend at public expense, 70 percent said they oppose it.

It is significant to note that public awareness of the Common Core State Standards is not only growing but that only a year later they are now on the radar screen of most Americans. In its annual survey of the public's attitudes toward the public schools, Phi Delta Kappan reported that public awareness of the Common Core Standards has increased from 38 percent in 2013 to 81 percent in 2014. In addition, 60 percent of Americans oppose requiring teachers in their community to use the Common Core State Standards to guide what they teach because many people fear it will limit the flexibility that teachers have to teach what they think is best (PDK/Gallup 2014, 11).

Further evidence of the pushback by the American people against the current education reform agenda was reported by Paul

Fallon in a statewide poll conducted in 2013 in Ohio. The results of his survey indicated that six out of ten of Ohio's registered voters believe students, teachers, and school districts should not be rated solely on test scores but also on other measures such as student grades, public engagement, and graduate success (Fallon 2013).

At the local level, opinion research, discussions with civic leaders, and informal conversations hosted by school district residents in Lorain County, Ohio, reinforce what PDK/Gallup and Fallon have learned about how citizens react when they become aware of the school reform initiatives impacting them and their public schools.

In September of 2013, Greg Ring attended two informal coffee conversations in Lorain County to discuss education reform measures that are in place in Ohio and how these reforms are impacting them and their local schools. Greg is superintendent of the Educational Service Center of Lorain County.

The individuals hosting each of the coffee conversations invited their guests by calling them personally and explaining the purpose for getting together. It is significant to note that all of the twenty-eight residents who were invited to attend these coffees thought the topic was important enough for them to show up. And when they showed up, they had a lot to say.

"Prior to attending these coffees, most of the guests said they had been unaware of the impact of the current education reform movement," Greg explained. "However, following both of our two-hour-long discussions, they acknowledged that, although they continued to support having higher educational standards, they were now concerned about the future of their public schools."

Greg also learned from these frank and open conversations that the loss of funds to vouchers and charter schools and keeping pace with state mandates and other changes in education policy are perceived by many people to be the greatest challenges facing our public schools. Some of the comments he heard include: "It sounds like they are trying to dissolve the public schools." "We are going to lose too many dollars to effectively sustain our schools." "The value of a free public education and willingness to support it is now at stake."

When Greg asked the coffee discussion guests what it would take for citizens to become more involved in determining the future of their public schools, one person stated what other people in the room were thinking: "People just need an invitation and will get involved if they feel that their input is really wanted and will count for something."

As result of these coffee conversations, the sixteen superintendents in Lorain County commissioned a telephone survey in January of 2014 to learn how residents throughout their county feel about their schools and the education reforms which have been mandated for their students and teachers. Here is what they heard from their communities:

- Seven out of ten residents believe their school districts are doing an excellent or good job.

- High-quality teachers are the most important indicator of a high-quality education—followed by college and career readiness and a comprehensive curriculum.

- It is not very important that their school districts earn high marks on the state report card.

- Two out of three respondents do not believe that increased state testing is helping students.

- Decisions are best made at the local level. Fewer than one out of three respondents think that policy decisions made at the state level are in the best interest of students.

- Three out of four residents support expanding preschool education, especially for students from poverty, and a majority of them said they would increase their taxes to support it.

- Six out of ten residents oppose using their local tax dollars to support for-profit and online charter schools and seven out of ten oppose vouchers going to support parochial and private schools.

Our innate need to make a difference

In the midst of the attack on 9/11 that ended 3,000 innocent lives, why did the American people drop what they were doing, put aside their differences, and contribute their time and money to help the families and friends of those who were killed and the residents of New York City deal with the crisis? Why do we always come together, open our wallets, roll up our sleeves, and fix the problem when faced with a natural disaster or a threat to our national security?

For the answer to the question of why Americans nearly always come through when they are called upon to make a difference, I draw upon the wisdom of two of my favorite writers and thinkers. One is Stephen Covey, and the other is David Mathews.

Abraham Maslow, Carl Rogers, and other leading psychologists have long agreed that one of our greatest psychological needs in life is the need to be valued. In his highly acclaimed book, *The Seven Habits of Highly Effective People*, Stephen Covey incorporates this fundamental concept about human nature into his Habit 5, "Seek first to understand, then be understood." In the foreword to the 2004 edition of his book, he explains that "few needs of the human heart are greater than the need to be understood—to have a voice that is heard, respected, and valued—have influence . . . The real beginning of influence comes as others sense you are being influenced by them—when they feel understood by you—that you have listened deeply and sincerely, and that you are open . . . Our culture cries out for, even demands, understanding and influence" (Covey 2004, 10).

Valuing our thinking and giving us an opportunity to make a difference not only contributes to our positive psychological health and well-being, it is also a key ingredient in what Kettering Foundation President David Mathews describes as our untapped reservoir of civic duty. In his book, *Politics for People: Finding a Responsible Public Voice*, Mathews asserts that most of us underestimate the deep sense of civic duty that lies behind all of the complaints and cynical comments that people make about politics. To the contrary, the American people are quite proud of their communities and their nation, and because they care, they struggle to make a difference in a political system that seems to have little room for them (Mathews 1999).

Mathews explains that "Americans usually understand that there can be no quick fixes when they think about the fundamental dysfunctions of the political system. They certainly have no illusions about how difficult it is for citizens to become involved and make a difference—even just to make their voices heard" (Mathews 1999, 39).

Reaching a tipping point

The convergence of these four powerful societal trends has set the stage for the American people to step up and make a difference for our nation's public schools. All that remains is for the level of public awareness to reach a tipping point.

In the classic story of "The Hundredth Monkey," Ken Keyes, an author and lecturer on personal growth, explains how reaching a tipping point works:

The Japanese monkey, Macaca Fuscata, had been observed

in the wild for a period of over thirty years. In 1952, on the island of Koshima, scientists were providing monkeys with sweet potatoes dropped in the sand. The monkeys liked the taste of the raw sweet potatoes, but they found the dirt unpleasant.

An eighteen-month-old female named Imo found she could solve the problem by washing the potatoes in a nearby stream. She taught this trick to her mother. Her playmates also learned this new way and they taught their mothers, too.

This cultural innovation was gradually picked up by various monkeys before the eyes of the scientists. Between 1952 and 1958 all the young monkeys learned to wash the sandy sweet potatoes to make them more palatable. Only the adults who imitated their children learned this social improvement. Other adults kept eating the dirty sweet potatoes.

Then something startling took place. In the autumn of 1958, a certain number of Koshima monkeys were washing sweet potatoes—the exact number is not known. Let us suppose that when the sun rose one morning there were ninety-nine monkeys on Koshima Island who had learned to wash their sweet potatoes. Let's further suppose that later that morning, the hundredth monkey learned to wash potatoes.

THEN IT HAPPENED!

By that evening almost everyone in the tribe was washing sweet potatoes before eating them. The added energy of this hundredth monkey somehow created an ideological breakthrough!

But notice: A most surprising thing observed by these scientists was that the habit of washing sweet potatoes then jumped over the sea. . . . Colonies of monkeys on other islands and the mainland troop of monkeys at Takasaki-yama began washing their sweet potatoes.

Thus, when a certain critical number achieves an awareness, this new awareness may be communicated from mind to mind.

Although the exact number may vary, this Hundredth Monkey Phenomenon means that when only a limited number of people know of a new way, it may remain the conscious property of these people. But there is a point at which if only one more person tunes in to a new awareness, a field is strengthened so that this awareness is picked up by almost everyone!

The Hundredth Monkey Phenomenon was validated in 2011 in a study entitled, "Minority Rules: Scientists Find the Tipping Point." In their study, researchers from the Rensselaer Polytechnic Institute discovered that in order to change the beliefs of an entire community, only 10 percent of the population needs to become convinced of a new or different opinion. At that tipping point, the idea can spread through social networks and alter behaviors on a large scale (Sohn 2011).

This study and "The Hundredth Monkey" story explain what I first observed in the West Holmes School District in 1995 when voters overwhelmingly approved a $10 million bond issue and what I have repeatedly witnessed in many other school districts over the past two decades. Through the tipping point process, a relatively small number of people can influence the thinking of an entire school district and even a nation.

I am confident that when the crisis facing our nation's education system reaches a tipping point and penetrates the threshold of public consciousness of the American people, they will do what they have always done when their help is needed. They will rise to the occasion and fix the problem.

In the next chapter, I provide evidence that this is already beginning to happen.

References

Covey, Stephen R. 2004. *The Seven Habits of Highly Effective People: Powerful Lessons in Personal Change.* Free Press edition, Simon & Schuster, New York.

Fallon, Paul. 2013. *Ohio Omnibus Survey, Fall 2013 Results.* Fallon Research & Communications, Inc.

Jones, Jeffrey M. 2013, December 18. "Record High in U.S. Say Big Government Greatest Threat." *Gallup Politics.* http://www.gallup.com/poll/166535/record-high-say-big-government-greatest-threat.aspx.

Keyes, Ken. 1982. *The Hundredth Monkey.* Camarillo, CA: Vision Books.

Mathews, David. 1999. *Politics for People: Finding a Responsible Public Voice.* Urbana, IL: University of Illinois Press.

McCarthy, Justin. 2014, June 30. "Americans Losing Confidence in All Branches of U.S. Gov't." *Gallup Politics.* http://www.gallup.com/poll/171992/americans-losing-confidence-branches-gov.aspx.

_____. 2014, April 10. "No Improvement for Congress' Job Approval Rating." *Gallup Politics.* http://www.gallup.com/poll/168428/no-improvement-congressional-approval.aspx.

PDK/Gallup. 2013. "45th Annual Phi Delta Kappan/Gallup Poll of the Public's Attitudes Toward the Public Schools." Kappan. http://www.oapcs.org/files/u1/2013_PDKGallup.pdf.

_____. 2014. "46th Annual Phi Delta Kappan/Gallup Poll of the Public's Attitudes Toward the Public Schools," *Kappan*. http://pdkintl.org/noindex/PDK_Poll46_2014.pdf.

Sohn, Emily. 2011, August 4. "Minority Rules: Scientists Find the Tipping Point." *Discovery News*. http://news.discovery.com/human/opinion-minority-rules-110804.htm.

Part V

Where We Go from Here

Today, a growing number of school superintendents are beginning to step up to the plate and sound the alarm that our nation's public schools are at a turning point. There is also evidence that the American people are ready to get involved and make a difference when they are provided with a little guidance on what they can do and how they can do it.

Chapter 18

Initial Attempts to Sound the Alarm

While much of the general public remains in the dark about what is happening to our nation's public schools, there is light at the end of the proverbial tunnel, and that light is fortunately not an oncoming train. Instead, it is emanating from a growing number of school superintendents who are engaging their communities in frank and open conversations about the impact of our country's education reform movement.

In this chapter, I share important stories about some of these initial attempts to sound the alarm that our public schools are at a turning point.

*   *   *

West Lafayette, Indiana

One Indiana superintendent of schools is not only making a difference for his school system and community, but he is also helping to change the national debate about education reform. His name is Rocky Killion, and he is spearheading an ambitious initiative to inform the American people how the education reform movement is impacting them and their schools.

Rise Above the Mark

To alert the general public about what he calls the "corporate takeover" of Indiana's public schools and let citizens know what they can do about it, Rocky—with the support of his Board of School Trustees, the West Lafayette Schools Education Foundation, and the administration and staff of the West Lafayette Community School Corporation—has produced an education documentary titled *Rise Above the Mark* (www.riseabovethemark.com).

One of the major messages from this documentary is that legislators and policymakers are trying to privatize our public schools by offering "school choice." In doing this, they are diverting public tax dollars from the public schools and giving them to corporations. If the public schools are dismantled, equal educational access for all children will disappear. The end result, if unchallenged, will cripple our society, destroy our economy, and create generations of impoverished children.

Another theme of *Rise Above the Mark* is that, as a nation, if we are interested in reforming public education, all Americans must first consider if the current education reforms are really working. The National Center on Education and the Economy indicates that many of the problems we face in public education are caused by our political system, not by educators. Legislators craft and pass educational legislation and then direct school boards and administrators to implement it. When their legislation doesn't work, school boards, educators, and administrators are generally blamed for the failure.

In Rocky's opinion, "If the United States is to have the best education system in the world, the political agendas must be removed from the equation. This does not mean that politics will never play a role in supporting our education system. What it does mean is that politicians and policymakers must nurture and support a public education system that empowers local boards, administrators, and educators to make educational decisions for their respective communities and then hold them accountable for their decisions."

The public's reaction

Since its premier on December 12, 2013, more than ten thousand people have seen *Rise Above the Mark*. Showings of the documentary have been hosted throughout the United States and in a number of countries around the world—including Belgium, Denmark, Finland, and the Netherlands.

When I asked Rocky about the public's reaction to the documentary, he told me, "Shock and awe." He explained that after viewing it, many people said that they hadn't been aware of what had been happening to our nation's public schools and then asked, "What can we help do about it?"

His response to them (Killion 2014) has been to contact their state's elected officials and ask them to:

- initiate education legislation that puts decision making for instruction, curriculum, and student testing back into the hands of local teachers, administrators, and school boards;
- invest in early childhood programs for all children;
- allow public schools the flexibility of implementing educator-driven initiatives that really help children learn rather than using a "one-size-fits-all" model of education reform;
- use standardized testing sparingly and only for diagnostic purposes;
- stop the diversion of general-fund dollars from the public schools to charter and private schools;
- return local control of the general fund back to our schools; and

- invest resources in our public schools so that all children, regardless of where they live, receive a high-quality education.

As a direct result of the documentary, a coalition of public schools is forming in Indiana to address the impact of the education reform measures being mandated upon them. The members of this coalition of local educational leaders plan to meet with their local citizens, discuss the challenges their teachers and students are facing, and ask them to share their views about the situation with their state officeholders.

With regard to the West Lafayette Community School Corporation, Rocky lays it on the line: "Legislators are calling the shots and putting our school system in an ever-shrinking box. We need to secure the resources and legislative relief necessary to achieve our school district's mission of creating a world-class educational system for all children. To turn our mission into reality, we need to put decision making back into the hands of our school board, educational staff, and community" (Killion 2014).

* * *

Grand Rapids, Michigan

Mike Paskewicz, superintendent of the Northview Public Schools in Grand Rapids, Michigan, has created an innovative way to help residents in his community shape the future of their schools. He is utilizing the power of the social media to build support for his school system and influence education policy in his state. Each week, he sends an e-mail chronicling "Every Day Evidence That Our Public Schools Are Working" to Michigan's governor and his local state legislators. In addition, he copies these e-mails to his 400 school employees and 350 opinion leaders in his community.

In a recent interview, Mike shared with me the details of his story and how it is making a difference.

What prompted you to create this "Every Day Evidence That Our Public Schools Are Working" communication strategy?

Mike: Prior to being appointed superintendent of the Northview Public Schools four years ago, I served as superintendent of two large school districts in Utah and Colorado. While there, I learned the value of building community coalitions and engaging school district residents in frank and open conversations about important issues and concerns facing their schools. Today, one of the most important questions that needs to be addressed is whether or not our public schools are working. Our district's "Every Day Evidence That Our Public Schools Are Working" initiative is my answer to this important question as it pertains to the Northview Public Schools.

What specifically did you do to kick off your initiative?

Mike: Actually, it was fairly simple. At our opening day of school this past year, I asked our staff to thank five people for doing something good for our students and to copy me. I explained that I would share their stories with our governor and state legislators. In addition, I said I would forward copies of my e-mails to our staff and opinion leaders in our community. It was amazing. I received dozens of examples of everyday evidence that our public schools work. What's more, today, I continue to receive three to four good news stories a week from our staff, students, parents, and others in the community.

How did you develop your list of community opinion leaders?

Mike: I utilized the mapping strategy that Jamie Vollmer included in his book *Schools Cannot Do It Alone*. In a nutshell, we asked a team of people who know our community to identify opinion leaders from civic clubs and organizations, fraternal societies, professional associations, labor organizations, ethnic societies, businesses, religious institutions, school-related groups and organizations, school-community partnerships, vendors, ad hoc assemblies, and virtual organizations. Now, every time I click the button on my computer, I can reach more than 750 important stakeholders.

Would you share the content of one of "Every Day Evidence" e-mail messages?

Mike: Of course. On February 18, 2013, I sent the following e-mail to our governor and state legislators and copied it to our staff and community opinion leaders (Paskewicz 2013):

> Dear Senator Jansen, Representatives MacGregor, Lyons, Hooker, Yonker, and VerHeulen, and Governor Snyder,
>
> One of our core beliefs is that we are all responsible for student success and learning. Today's "Every Day Evidence That Our Public Schools Are Working" highlights an e-mail thank you to our teachers from Aaron Oom. Aaron graduated from Northview in 2012 and was accepted to Michigan State University Honors College on a full-ride academic scholarship:
>
> *Dr. Paskewicz,*
>
> *I just wanted to send you an e-mail letting you know how much I appreciate the math and science programs at Northview. I took math up through Calculus I at Northview and have taken Calculus II and III here at Michigan State University. The first*

few weeks or so of Calculus II were essentially review for me thanks to the fantastic teaching of Tina Ely.

The work I've been doing in Calculus III has been firmly rooted in the foundation Northview laid out for me over the years, making it substantially easier to learn new material. I think it should be noted that I transferred into this class about three weeks late and was caught up within a short period of time after getting some help here. But the material I learned in AP Physics, taught by Erin Combs, Calculus I, and Algebra I & II, taught by Matt Coty and Becky Fase respectively, gave me the necessary background to catch up easily with only a small amount of help.

I'm also enrolled in Physics II here at State and I would be remiss if I didn't mention that AP Physics did a sterling job of preparing me for the class. I learned everything I needed to in AP Physics to be ready for the second semester of college physics. I have never had a point where I needed to go back and learn something from Physics I that I didn't learn in order to move on with Physics II.

As a biochemistry major I am required to take basic chemistry and after taking AP Chemistry, taught by Jim Haveman, and Honors Chemistry, taught by Brian Kammers, I have been well prepared to go more in depth here at MSU.

Finally, I work on campus in a lab doing cancer research through cell culture technique and while at times I am thoroughly baffled by the complicated topics we're investigating, I have some background in cellular biology thanks to AP Biology, taught by Brian Bollone, and Biology, taught by Brian Hendricks. This background has given me a great starting point for discussing the work I do. I have been also able to have an understanding of the basic statistical analysis we use for data thanks to Chip Aymer who taught the elementary statistics course I took my senior year.

I am truly thankful for each and every one of these fantastic teachers and the foundations they have laid for me. They helped to sustain my passion for math and science, and for that I am truly thankful.

This e-mail from Aaron is a good example of our staff's strong commitment to student learning and success. It also demonstrates what occurs when our teachers are not over-burdened by government-mandated rules and regulations and have the time and flexibility required to meet the individual educational needs of their students.

Sincerely,
Mike Paskewicz, Superintendent
Northview Public Schools

How do you know if this "Every Day Evidence" strategy is working?

Mike: This is a great question. To me, the most important result of this initiative is the positive impact it is having on our staff. Our school employees thank me on a regular basis for supporting them, and they are sharing the e-mails with their Facebook and other social media friends. Another indicator that it is working comes from my daily contact with school district residents. Each week, I talk with residents who tell me they have shared or received one of my e-mails.

Why do the "every day evidence that our schools work" stories seem to be going viral?

Mike: I think there are a couple of reasons. First, they are heartfelt and authentic. Secondly, the direct recipient of these stories are the governor and our state legislators. Our staff and community opinion leaders are receiving these e-mails indirectly as an FYI. In essence, they are being given inside information that is going from me to our political leaders.

This approach is very different from the typical way many superintendents share good news with their communities.

Mike: Yes, it is. In fact, I think you've hit upon a major reason why this FYI approach seems to be working so well. In today's environment, many people are suspicious of anyone trying to sell them anything and that includes good news about our schools. It is probably why the persuasive power of school newsletters is limited. However, sharing "inside information" directed to our governor and state legislators sends a message to our staff and community opinion leaders that we trust them, and it provides them with insight to which they would not normally be privy.

Are your e-mails having any influence on your state's political leaders?

Mike: While the jury is out with regard to a definitive answer to this question, there is strong evidence that it is having a positive impact. For example, 170 parents from our school system and other school districts in our county attended a workshop to help them influence education policy in our state. In addition, I recently spoke with one of our state legislators who told me that phone calls and e-mails from school parents and other school district residents are increasing.

Have there been any surprises?

Mike: Yes. I've been impressed with how powerful the social media are as a vehicle for initiating conversation on a broad scale. The message that our schools are working is beginning to resonate beyond our community. For example, Friends of Kent County Schools has recently been formed by concerned parents in the Grand Rapids area and is working with other parents throughout Michigan to help shape education policy in our state.

What advice do you have for anyone thinking about replicating what you are doing?

Mike: In my thirty-seven years in education, I've never seen anything close to what is going on today. I truly believe that a concerted effort is underway to dismantle our public schools and privatize public education. With that said, my advice to anyone thinking about replicating what we are doing in our school district is to try it for ninety days. Once you start doing it and begin to see the positive results from your effort, it will become a habit and take on a life of its own.

*   *   *

Lorain County, Ohio

When Greg Ring served as superintendent of the Firelands Local School District in Lorain County, Ohio, he learned up close and personally how citizens will put their differences aside and work together when the educational needs of their children are on the line. He learned what I have repeatedly discovered throughout my career—the American people want to be asked to help make important decisions impacting them and their schools.

Greg's journey of self-reflection and insight began when he faced an impending and potentially divisive decision regarding his school district's finances and had to decide how to approach the situation. What he ultimately did was challenge the conventional wisdom about how to pass a school tax increase.

Instead of placing an operating levy on the ballot and then trying to sell it to the voters, he and his board of education first discussed the situation with the residents of their school district. Over a six-month period, he attended more than thirty coffee conversations in homes throughout the Firelands School District. The only exception was a discussion with twenty antitax farmers held in a barn—which turned out to be one of the most productive meetings he attended.

When he was named superintendent of the Lorain County Educational Service Center, he brought with him what he learned about the power of engaging the American people in meaningful discussions about important issues. Currently, he is leading an initiative to help residents in the county gain local control of their schools.

Local control

As I discussed in the previous chapter, in January of 2014 Greg and the sixteen superintendents in Lorain County, Ohio, commissioned a telephone survey to gauge the public's perception of their schools, policies, and practices. The results of the county-wide survey clearly showed that the majority of residents in Lorain County oppose most of the education reforms being imposed on their school systems by their state's policymakers and that they want more local control of their schools.

Below is the public response from Lorain County's superintendents to what they heard (Ring 2014):

- The vast majority of citizens in our county are unaware of the reforms being mandated by their education policymakers in Columbus and Washington, DC.
- We superintendents are much to blame for not standing up to these ill-fated education reforms.
- Our overriding concern is the loss of local control of our public schools.
- Other major related concerns include the impact of the third grade reading guarantee, the appropriateness of the PARCC assessments (the high-stakes tests to be taken by students to determine how well they are meeting the benchmarks

of the Common Core Standards) and our preparedness to implement them, the integrity of the Ohio teacher evaluation growth measures, the lack of accountability of Ohio's charter schools, and the lack of state support for preschool education.

- Over the next several months, we will be talking with our communities about solutions we are proposing to address each of these concerns and about other issues that our citizens feel need to be discussed.
- In order to take back local control of our schools, we will need to engage our communities in meaningful conversations about proposed school reform initiatives before they become law—which is why we will be asking our boards of education to consider passing a resolution to return local control to our public schools.

By June of 2013, all of the school boards in Lorain County had passed the following resolution:

A resolution to return local control

Whereas, by the beginning of the twentieth century, America's leaders began to shift nonacademic duties to our nation's public schools.

Whereas, in 1983 in response to the report (*A Nation at Risk*) that our schools were failing, our nation's leaders accelerated the ever-increasing burden being placed upon our public schools by mandating more educational changes.

Whereas, these mandates include the siphoning of nearly $1 billion in tax dollars from Ohio's public schools into for-profit, online, and other charter schools, increasing the reliance on high-stakes testing to measure the worth of our public schools and reducing our ability to provide our students with a balanced education.

Whereas, additionally, these mandates place an unfair burden on our teachers by judging their performance based largely on one high-stakes test and increase government control while decreasing local control of our schools.

Whereas, based upon the results of a county-wide survey conducted in January 2014, the majority of residents in Lorain County feel connected to their local public schools, believe their schools are doing a good job of preparing their students for the future, think that having high quality teachers is the most important indicator of high quality education.

Whereas, the survey further showed that residents do not support many of the state and federal school reform mandates that are impacting them and their local school systems.

Whereas, the majority of residents in Lorain County believe that increased state testing has not helped students, that student test scores from one standardized test should not be used to evaluate teacher performance, that their tax dollars should not be used to support vouchers for profit and online charter schools, that education policy decisions made at the state level are not in the best interest of our students and that there should not be more state/federal government control over our public schools.

Whereas, the vast majority of citizens, however, are unaware of the scope and impact of how these educational mandates (especially those that are unfunded) are impacting them and their public schools.

Therefore, it is time to return local control to our public schools by asking our state legislators in Lorain County to draft legislation requiring Ohio's citizens to have an opportunity to review and discuss changes in education policy before they turn into educational mandates.

Planting the seeds for a statewide initiative

On March 25, 2014, Greg Ring and six other Ohio superintendents met with Kirk Hamilton, executive director of the Buckeye Association of School Administrators and shared with him what Lorain County was doing to inform parents and other community members about the impact of the Common Core Standards and other educational reforms. BASA is the statewide organization representing most of Ohio's school superintendents.

Steve Barrett, one of the superintendents who also attended our March meeting at BASA, discussed what he had done during the past year to inform his school parents and community about the impact of the Common Core Standards. He explained that while most of them supported the basic goals of the new standards, some of them expressed concern about the student testing, the selection of reading materials, and other aspects of how the standards would be implemented.

Following our meeting with Kirk, Greg and some of his Lorain County colleagues attended several regional meetings of superintendents throughout the state and shared with them the details of their Lorain County initiative. Not surprisingly, the idea of empowering their citizens to help them restore some semblance of local control of their schools resonated with many of the superintendents who participated in these regional meetings.

Three months later, Kirk hosted a follow-up meeting to discuss the feedback from the regional superintendent meetings and to decide what, if any, next steps should be taken. Following a two-hour discussion, the decision was made to invite Rocky Killion to present his documentary, *Rise Above the Mark*, with Ohio's superintendents and to utilize the occasion as a catalyst to engage the citizens of Ohio in a statewide conversation about the impact of education reform on both them and their schools.

*   *   *

Texas High Performance Schools Consortium

To help improve student learning in the state's public school system, in September 2012, Texas Commissioner of Education Michael Williams formed the Texas High Performance Schools Consortium. Comprised of twenty-three school districts representing a wide range of district types, sizes, and diverse student populations, the Consortium focused its attention on digital learning, high priority learning standards, multiple assessments, and community involvement.

"The school districts selected to participate in the consortium are already known for their innovative work and are looked to by many as educational leaders. This exciting project will help the Governor, legislative leaders, and the Texas Education Agency craft a sound, well-thought out plan to move all Texas schools to the next performance level," Williams said (Williams 2012).

In addition to their focus on teaching and learning, the superintendents who comprised the consortium were strongly committed to seeking ways to involve their staff members, parents, and communities in the important decisions regarding the education of their children. And they acted upon that commitment by immediately addressing a major problem impacting their students.

Grassroots effort

In Texas, the proliferation of high-stakes tests being given to students had reached a saturation point. To address the problem, the consortium reached out to its member communities and asked for help. As a result of an outpouring of grassroots support from school parents, teachers, and community leaders, Texas lawmakers overwhelmingly passed legislation to reduce the amount of high-stakes testing.

Prior to passage of the legislation, high school students were taking up to fifteen multiple-choice accountability tests in a single year. This legislation reduced the number of tests to five. In addition to the number of hours students were spending taking tests, teachers and staff in the Lewisville Independent School District, for example, spent 4,392 hours during the 2011–2012 school year receiving training on the distribution of the new tests, coordinating the delivery of tests, or proctoring tests.

Finally, the icing on the cake was that these tests were not important for the college admissions process. In essence, students were spending much of their high school careers taking tests, most of which were not based upon college readiness standards and were not useful for college nor aligned to any career field.

In 2013, the grassroots effort by citizens in the twenty-three districts that comprised the Texas High Performance Schools Consortium also led to the passage of another bill that would have reduced the number of accountability tests for Texas' elementary and middle school students. The governor, however, vetoed the legislation.

Next steps

In talking with some of the leaders of the consortium, they told me they are gratified at the amount of public support these two legislative initiatives received. One superintendent reported that advocates for the initiatives included a wide array of diverse groups and organizations which ranged from the teachers' unions to the Tea Party.

Next steps for the consortium members will be to invite other school districts to join them in their work and to continue reaching out to the citizens of Texas and getting them involved in the important decisions regarding the education of their children.

*   *   *

The personal stories that I have just shared are not exclusive to Indiana, Michigan, Ohio, and Texas. They are also being written in many other states.

By the time this book is published, the number of citizens who are aware of how the education reform movement is impacting their schools and are doing something about it will have grown. In the next chapter, I lay out a practical strategy for what we can do as individual citizens to create our own stories to help shape the future of our nation's public schools.

References

Killion, Rocky. 2014. *Rise Above the Mark: Public Education Reforms That Work.* West Lafayette, IN: West Lafayette School Corporation. DVD, 65 min.

Paskewicz, Mike. 2013. "Every Day Evidence That Our Public Schools Are Working," Northview Public Schools e-mail.

Ring, Greg. 2014. "What's Best for Lorain County's Schools?" Educational Service Center of Lorain County, Elyria, Ohio. http://www.restorelocalcontrol.org/whats-best-for-lorain-county.html.

Williams, Michael. 2012, September 19. "23 Districts Selected High Performance Schools Consortium members." *Texas Education Agency News.*

Chapter 19

What We Can Do as Individual Citizens

One of my favorite quotes is attributed to the American cultural anthropologist Margaret Mead who reportedly said: "Never doubt that a small group of thoughtful, committed citizens can change the world. Indeed, it is the only thing that ever has."

Her quote captures the essence of what I have learned about the powerful influence that a small group of thoughtful, committed citizens can have when the educational needs of their schoolchildren are at stake. Time and time again, I have seen fewer than a dozen people rally the members of their community to pass a tax increase for their schools or make other kinds of difficult decisions.

In this chapter, I am going to discuss what you and some of your friends can do as thoughtful, committed citizens to help spark a movement in your community, state, and, ultimately, our nation to help shape the future of our public schools. I will begin by briefly revisiting the explanation for how a small group of people, like yourselves, can influence the thinking of an entire school district or even "change the world" and then describe two conditions that need to be present in order to provide the emotional energy to initiate and sustain this movement.

For the past twenty-five years, I have spent a significant portion of my career trying to figure out how to help the American people shape the future of their schools. With a lot of help from many of my superintendent colleagues, we have tested and built community engagement strategies that have proven to be both practical and successful. For the remainder of this chapter, I will explain, step by step, how you can utilize these strategies to get involved and make a difference.

How a small group of people can change the world

As I explained in chapter 17, only a small portion of the population needs to become convinced of a new or different opinion or behavior for it to spread through social networks and alter opinions or behaviors on a large scale. The exact point at which it begins to spread is called the tipping point.

In the 1952 study of the Japanese monkeys, the tipping point was the hundredth monkey. In their study in 2011, researchers from the Rensselaer Polytechnic Institute discovered that in order to change the beliefs of an entire community, only 10 percent of the population needs to become convinced of a new or different opinion.

Two conditions that need to be present

Two conditions are needed to successfully initiate and sustain a movement as ambitious and important as shaping the future of our schools. One is a sense of urgency that needs to be addressed, and the other is providing citizens with an opportunity to talk among themselves and not just with their school officials and other community leaders.

For the past two decades, I have been conducting workshops on how to build community support for passing school tax issues and making other important decisions involving our nation's public schools. At the beginning of every workshop, I make the following statement:

"If you take away only one thing from today's workshop, please listen carefully to what I am about to tell you. In order to pass a tax issue, the need for public support must be urgent, and it must be clearly communicated. Most tax issues fail, not because of a lack of trust, but because of a lack of a sense of urgency."

The remainder of each workshop is devoted to discussing how to engage citizens in frank and open dialogue about what is at stake and what they can do about it. I stress that this dialogue needs to be among the citizens themselves, not just with school officials. This is an extremely important point that is often missed when school leaders think about how to best discuss issues and concerns with their residents. Instead of serving as a forum for an open exchange of ideas and concerns with and among community members, school-led discussions typically end up being question-and-answer sessions with the superintendent and school board members.

One of the insights from the work of the Kettering Foundation is that some of the most helpful discussions people can have are those where they can explore the nature of problems and the opinions of others—meetings where they can say to one another, "I don't have a clue to what you are talking about; can you explain?" (Mathews 1999, 41). Kettering Foundation President David Mathews states that Americans are unhappy that most public dialogue isn't really a dialogue:

> People who attend forums say that they want to talk together—to hear and to be heard.
>
> They don't just want to be lectured (to) or addressed ... Talking together, not just talking, is the heart of a public discussion. When people talk, they learn about issues, exchange ideas, and even change their perspectives ... Through discussion, people begin to see beyond their private interests and find interests they have in

common. They begin to develop informed judgments on issues … Informed judgment provides the foundation of common purpose needed for both citizens and government action (Mathews 1999, 45).

How to make it happen

For the remainder of this chapter, I will provide you with specific ideas and, in some instances, step-by-step processes for what you can do as an individual citizen to reclaim responsibility for your schools and help shape the future of education reform.

Step 1—Become aware of what is happening.

- As the saying goes, knowledge is power. Since you have reached this point in the book, you have already begun the important journey of becoming aware of what is happening to our country's education system. Here are several additional books that shine a bright light on this important topic:

  » *Schools Cannot Do It Alone: Building Support for America's Public Schools,* by Jamie Vollmer
  » *The Death and Life of the Great American School System: How Testing and Choice Are Undermining Education,* by Diane Ravitch
  » *Reign of Error: The Hoax of the Privatization Movement and the Danger to America's Public Schools,* by Diane Ravitch
  » *The School Reform Landscape: Fraud, Myth and Lies,* by Cristopher H. Tienken and Donald C. Orlich
  » *50 Myths & Lies That Threaten America's Public Schools: The Real Crisis in Education,* by David C. Berliner and Gene V. Glass
  » *Politics For People: Finding a Responsible Public Voice,* by David Mathews

- Purchase the Blu-ray HD or DVD of the powerful and enlightening documentary *Rise Above the Mark*. It is available online at RiseAbovetheMark.com.

- Schedule a one-on-one meeting with your superintendent of schools and discuss how the education reform movement is impacting your school district's students and teachers.

Step 2—Share this information with people you know.

- Lend this book to a friend, relative, or work associate.

- Lend the *Rise Above the Mark* documentary to someone you know.

- Invite a few friends to your home to preview the *Rise Above the Mark* documentary and suggest they follow up by reading this book.

- Preview *Rise Above the Mark* with groups and organizations to which you belong and suggest they follow up by reading this book.

Step 3—Form a book study group.

- Volunteer to help organize a book study group to read and discuss this book. Discussion questions are included in the appendix to this book.

- To kick off your book study, invite your study group to your home and preview the *Rise Above the Mark* documentary.

- Following initial discussions among yourselves, invite your superintendent to meet with your group to discuss how the education reform movement is impacting your teachers, students, and community.

Step 4—Host a coffee discussion in your home.

Nothing is more fulfilling, therapeutic, democratic, and powerful than sitting in a friend's living room with ten to fifteen other citizens from your community and discussing important issues and concerns. Since most coffee discussions are held in someone's home and the guests are the acquaintances of the host or hostess, the setting for the discussion is nearly always friendly, respectful, open, and inclusive. Here are the steps you can take to host a coffee discussion:

- First, determine the purpose of your coffee discussion. To accomplish this, there are a couple of approaches you can take. If the people you will be inviting to attend your coffee are, for the most part, unaware of how the education reform movement is impacting them and their schools, you may want to utilize your coffee as an opportunity to introduce them to this vitally important situation. Previewing the *Rise Above the Mark* documentary is a good way to kick off this initial discussion. The second approach you can take in hosting your coffee is to invite people you know who have had an opportunity to read this book or view the documentary and, as a result, possess some level of awareness and understanding about what is going on.

- Schedule a date and time for your coffee discussion. Usually, Monday through Thursday are the best days, and 7:00 or 7:30 p.m. is the best time of day. Many people are at work during the day, and most want to keep their weekends open for rest, relaxation, and family events.

- Once you have scheduled your coffee, create a guest list of fifteen to twenty people you know. They can be friends, neighbors, relatives, or work associates. And it doesn't make any difference whether or not they are school supporters. A diversity of views will enhance the authenticity of your coffee discussion.

- The key to getting people to show up at your coffee is to personally call them and ask them to attend. Once you have their personal commitment to show up, chances are very high that they will do it because, if they don't, they know they'll have to face you the next time they see you. A word of advice: Don't bother passing out invitation flyers in your neighborhood because they will not generate much, if any, attendance at your coffee.

- If I were going to invite people to attend my coffee discussion, this is what I would say: "Is this a good time to talk with you? (If yes, continue. If no, ask when would be a better time to talk.) To put it bluntly, I need your help. Diane and I are hosting a small group of friends in our home to talk about the future of our nation's education system and I need for you to be there. Our schools today are facing a number of critically important challenges and we, as American citizens, need to have a strong voice in what happens to them. Can I count on you to join us?" (If yes, thank the person and provide the date, time, and street location.) I would then follow up my call with a personal note thanking each person for their willingness to take time from their busy schedule to participate in what will be a very important discussion about the future of our country's education system.

- Here is an example of a coffee discussion agenda that you might be able to use:

Welcome and self-introductions	10 minutes

(Suggestion: Thank everyone for coming and get them involved right away by going around the room and asking each guest to introduce themselves and share why they were willing to take time from their schedule to attend the coffee discussion and what they hope to learn from it. One more thing: make sure you have everyone's e-mail addresses so you can stay in touch with them regarding future discussions and other opportunities to have a voice in determining the fate of our nation's public schools.)

Preview the *Rise Above the Mark* documentary	60 minutes
Follow the documentary by an open discussion focusing on the question: What is your reaction to what you just viewed?	40 minutes
Conclude by a discussion of what should be the next step or steps	10 minutes

(Here are some ideas: Have everyone purchase the documentary, join a book study discussion of *America's Schools at a Turning Point*, invite their superintendent of schools to meet with them and share how education reform is impacting their schools and community, and host their own coffee discussion.)

- On the next page, I have included some ground rules for a productive coffee discussion. Do not hand them out or review them with your guests at your coffee discussion. They don't need to be lectured about how to behave. Also, do not allow yourself to get bogged down in the task of trying to implement all of these ground rules. They are simply some tips for you to think about as you prepare to host your coffee discussion.

Ground Rules for a Productive Conversation

Have a "kitchen table" conversation.
Everyone participates.
No one dominates.

There are no "right" answers.
Draw on your own experiences, views, and beliefs.
You do not need to be an expert.

Keep an open mind.
Listen carefully.
Try to understand the views of those who disagree with you.

Help keep the discussion on track.
Stick to the questions.
Try not to ramble.

It is okay to disagree.
But don't be disagreeable.
Respond to others how you want to be responded to.

Have fun!
Collaborating is a rewarding experience.
It enables all of us to be of value and make a difference.

Adapted by the Santa Rita Collaborative from the Community Conversation Workbook, published in 2004 by the KnowledgeWorks Foundation and the Harwood Institute for Public Innovation.

Step 5—Let your elected representatives know what you are doing.

In the United States, when all is said and done, having a voice in determining education policy ultimately means having the ear of our elected representatives. In today's toxic political environment, some believe that only the loudest and most confrontational voices get heard. I disagree.

I believe that the American people are sick and tired of the political fighting, grandstanding, and gridlock. I also believe that many, if not most, of our elected representatives feel the same way. As a result, the timing is now right for everyone to sit down and have a reasoned and respectful conversation about the future of our education system and other serious challenges facing our country.

Throughout this book, I have shared numerous examples of how shedding our political labels, focusing on what really matters, and working together to address the educational needs of our children not only works, but works like a charm. I believe this is how to get things done and, if you intend to follow this path, let your elected representatives know about it. Most of them will not only appreciate it, but they will perceive it to be a breath of fresh air and embrace it.

With this said, here are some ideas for letting your elected representatives know what you are doing to reclaim responsibility for your schools:

- Write a personal letter of introduction and send it to your state representative, state senator, governor, US representative, and two US senators. Their names, addresses, and phone numbers are available online. In your letter, let them know that you are concerned about how some aspects of the education reform movement are impacting your schools and community and explain what you are doing (organizing a book study group, hosting a coffee discussion, etc.) to get involved in helping shape future education reforms. Also, ask them what they feel are the greatest challenges facing them and how you can help them deal with these challenges. While an e-mail is better than nothing, a handwritten letter will have the greatest impact.

- Follow up your letter of introduction by scheduling a one-on-one meeting with them and their staff who, in many instances, serve as their gatekeeper. The purpose of scheduling this meeting is twofold. One is to let them know who you are by putting your face with your name. The other is to reinforce how serious you are about reclaiming responsibility for your schools. Although it may be a bit of a challenge to schedule meetings with your governor and two US senators, it should be relatively easy for you to schedule them with your state representative, state senator, and US representative. You will be able to meet with them when they are at their offices at your state capital or in Washington, DC, or when they are back home in your district.

- Once you establish a personal relationship with your elected officials and they perceive you to be knowledgeable, supportive, and reasonable, you have put yourself into a good position for them to listen to you.

Step 6—Ask your superintendent to help keep you informed.

- Ask your superintendent to include you on his or her e-mail list to update you on education policy initiatives that, if approved by the state or federal government, will impact you and your local schools.

- Also, suggest to your superintendent that his or her teaching staff periodically host teacher panel discussions to update you and your community on what is happening in the class-room.

• When education policy proposals are urgent, on a fast track, and need to be discussed quickly by the entire community, ask your superintendent and board of education to host a district-wide public meeting to talk about it. Make sure that tabletop discussions are included in the format of the meeting so the meeting doesn't become a question-and-answer session, and citizens are able to talk among themselves.

Step 7—Have faith that your voice can and will make a difference.

Earlier in my career, I worked as a political consultant for candidates seeking state and federal office and as a government relations executive for a Fortune 500 corporation. One of the most important things I learned from this experience is that our elected officials clearly understand they will not get elected or reelected if they fail to listen to their constituents. As a result, it is in their best interest to accurately measure the pulse of public opinion of those they are elected to represent.

While it is true that our elected officials sometimes respond to the loud and influential voices of special interest groups when they make important policy decisions, it is not always the case. In fact, more often than you might think, they seek the authentic voices of ordinary citizens which signal how the majority of their constituents really feel.

This is why your elected officials will listen to you, and it is why you need to have faith that your voice can and will make a difference.

For help in getting started

There is a commonly used saying that the first step in doing something new is always the most challenging one. For many, if not most, Americans, hosting a coffee discussion in their home about the future of their schools is a new experience.

If you are entertaining the idea of hosting a coffee discussion and have any questions or concerns, please do not hesitate to contact me. You can get in touch with me through my website: CorkyOCallaghan.com.

I look forward to hearing from you and will be sure to get back to you promptly.

References

Mathews, David. 1999. *Politics for People: Finding a Responsible Public Voice.* Urbana, IL: University of Illinois Press.

Chapter 20

A Beacon of Hope

This book is about more than education. It is about the good in America and why that goodness serves as a beacon of hope for our country's future.

Although the book's primary focus is the growing need for the American people to help shape the future of our public schools, the messages contained in the preceding chapters resonate beyond education. They tell an inspiring story about the goodness, decency, and compassion that resides within the American spirit. In this chapter, I will begin with the story of a young Frenchman who came to the United States and captured the essence of that spirit.

In 1831, the French government sent twenty-seven-year-old Alexis de Tocqueville to America to study and report on the American prison system. He traveled across our nation making notes not only on the prison systems but on all aspects of American society and government. From these notes Tocqueville wrote *Democracy in America*.

In his final campaign address in Boston, Massachusetts, in November 3, 1952, Dwight D. Eisenhower referred to one of Tocqueville's most powerful and often-used quotes:

I sought for the greatness and genius of America in her

commodious harbors and her ample rivers—and it was not there . . . in her fertile fields and boundless forests—and it was not there . . . in her rich mines and her vast world commerce—and it was not there . . . in her democratic Congress and her matchless Constitution—and it was not there. Not until I went into the churches of America and heard her pulpits flame with righteousness did I understand the secret of her genius and power. America is great because she is good, and if America ever ceases to be good, she will cease to be great.

Throughout my life, I have observed this goodness. However, upon reflection, it seems to me that the good in America rests not so much in our nation's institutions but in the hearts and minds of the American people themselves—the silent majority of citizens who care for one another and support one another when they are needed. I experienced this spirit of caring and support at a young age.

Growing up

When I was five years old, my parents and younger brother and I moved to a small community surrounded by farmland and located twelve miles north of Dayton, Ohio. Known at one time as the home of the world's largest manufacturer of lightning rods, the village of West Milton was safe, quiet, and full of people who cared about one another.

As children, my brother and I were able to ride our bicycles anywhere in town at any time of the day without fear of being harmed. We always felt safe. In fact, we never bothered locking the doors to either our home or car.

If we ran into a problem, someone would always call our parents and let them know we needed help because nearly everyone in town knew our family. One incident in which a neighbor came to our rescue involved a pet crow. I was nine years old at the time.

As my younger brother and I were making our daily trip to the local grocery store during our summer break from school, we spotted a large crow standing quietly in the middle of the street. Not having any fear of birds, we approached the bird and began to pet it.

Then, suddenly without warning, it flew up into one of the large maple trees that lined the street and started to dive-bomb us. It is not an overstatement to say that we feared for our lives. To protect ourselves, we lay prone on the street with our hands over our heads as this gigantic-looking bird flew menacingly within inches of us. Only later did we learn that the crow, named Freddy, was someone's pet.

I finally sent my brother for help, and thanks to one of our next door neighbors who happened to be sitting on her front porch, we were saved. She ran to where I was still lying prone with my hands over my head, diverted Freddy's attention, and escorted us safely home.

The point I want to make about our encounter with Freddy is that if it had not been our neighbor coming to our rescue, it would have been someone else in town performing what we perceived at the time to be a heroic act. And it would not have mattered if they had even known us because West Milton was the kind of community where people cared for one another and supported one another when they were needed.

For the record, we later learned from Freddy's owner that he wasn't really trying to hurt us. He was just playing with us. Nevertheless, it took several years into my adulthood for me to get over my fear of birds.

While everything wasn't perfect for me growing up, for the most part, I was very fortunate to have lived an *Ozzie and Harriet* kind of life in this friendly little town and to have experienced the goodness of its people. However, thankfully, my personal story of why America is good doesn't end here.

Throughout my career

For the past twenty-five years, I have repeatedly seen the ability of the American people to draw upon their innate goodness to triumph over the anger, frustration, divisiveness, and disillusionment that taints our politically driven culture. I would like to share one more story to illustrate how the good which dwells in the hearts and minds of the American people overcame a major loss of faith and confidence in one our nation's most trusted professions—our teachers.

Having conducted dozens of community opinion surveys throughout my career, I've found that teachers nearly always rank at the top of the list when citizens are asked what they like most about their local schools. So, as you might imagine, there is little more damaging to the spirit of a community than a teacher strike.

The reason why a strike can be so devastating to a community is that teachers are held in such high esteem by the majority of Americans and, when they go on strike, it is perceived by many people to be a breach of faith. In addition, since many community members know these teachers, this breach of faith becomes personal.

In late November of 1995, teachers in the Hillsdale Local School District, located in central Ohio, began a nine-day strike. Joel Roscoe, Hillsdale's superintendent of schools, tells the story of how he drew upon the goodness of his school employees, parents and the community to heal the emotional wounds caused by the strike:

> Hillsdale is a small district of 1,200 students. The school system is the center of the community and controversy concerning the schools quickly becomes everybody's business. The strike splintered the community, confusing some and infuriating others.

The issue was clearly not resolved when the teachers returned to their classrooms. As superintendent, I realized that actions had to be taken to rebuild the district and bring the community back to the schools. It was obvious that it would take time. And it was just as obvious that a sincere effort from everyone in this community was needed if the wounds created by the strike were ever to be mended.

The first attempt to heal was to personally welcome all of the teachers back to their classrooms. I went into every classroom and interrupted instruction (something I normally never do) to shake hands with the teachers and tell them I was glad they were back. I'll admit that this was not easy for me to do, and it was awkward for some of the staff as well, but it was an effort to reconnect that I think was appreciated.

The school board also offered to work with the teachers' association to develop a forum for communication based upon a labor-management model that would hopefully foster open dialogue. A conscious effort to acknowledge staff members and their efforts to improve instructional methods and other aspects of their professional development was increased through awards presented at the opening day of school and other forms of recognition made during National Teacher Week.

A major concern of the board of education was how to reconnect the schools with the community. To accomplish this, we developed a plan of action that embodied a community-based approach to planning for the future. This plan, however, required school staff to first determine educational needs that existed in the district which impaired their ability to effectively instruct children.

The first few meetings called to introduce the process were tentative at best. Many of us were simply not comfortable with opening up and letting everyone know how we really felt. Finally, during the third meeting, the ice was broken when a physical education teacher blurted out that bricks were falling from the wall of the gymnasium at the middle school and that she was concerned for her students' safety. That comment opened the gates for others to express legitimate concerns about safety and other issues that generated strong feelings among the staff.

Problems such as inadequate space to store science and math materials, poor ventilation in science labs, rooms with only one or two electrical outlets for computers, and the inadequate size of the middle school gym began to surface. These were concerns that had been suppressed for many years, and they were concerns that focused on the educational needs of children. I could feel at this point that the idea of opening up with one another and laying real concerns on the table was going to work.

After several more meetings, the staff developed build-ing-level lists which were then organized into recurring themes . . . A team of staff members from each building presented its concerns to the school board during a board work session. The atmosphere was not confrontational. Rather, it developed into an open dialogue of discovery with questions and comments relating to the children in our school district.

We have completed our second meeting with parents. In sharing their concerns about the educational needs of their buildings, the teachers presented a powerful message that *help is needed*. The response from parents has been open and sincere. For me, one of the most interesting insights from that meeting is that parents are not accus-tomed to being asked for their input. As one father put it, "So, what is it you think we should do?" I kindly reminded him that there is no master plan yet. I said, "That is why we are meeting."

It is naïve to imagine that the turmoil of a nine-day strike can be overcome in three months. It cannot. Nevertheless, we feel we are on the right track (O'Callaghan 1999).

Getting our country on the right track

Like the challenge that was facing the school administration, teachers, parents, and other community members in the Hillsdale Local School District, today the American people are facing the challenge of getting our country back on the right track.

According to a national telephone survey conducted by Rasmussen Reports of likely US voters in July of 2014, only 25 percent think our country is heading in the right direction. Sixty-seven percent of voters think the country is headed down the wrong track.

The number who say the country is heading in the right direction has been less than 30 percent for nineteen out of twenty-seven weeks in 2014. In 2013, 27 percent said the country was headed in the right direction, while 64 percent said it was going down the wrong track (Rasmussen Reports 2014).

Paraphrasing the words of Hillsdale's superintendent of schools, it is naïve to imagine that the pessimism about the direction of our country can be overcome overnight—or even in the near term. Over the past several years, public concern, and, for some, even anger and cynicism over the inability of our federal government to solve the major problems facing our country has become deeply rooted in the American psyche.

As I put the finishing touches on this book, these unresolved problems appear to be reaching a crisis point. As a nation, we are currently facing serious challenges with potentially dire consequences both at home and abroad. Externally, our personal health and safety are being threatened by a worldwide movement of terrorists who would like to kill us, while internally we are fighting our own not-so-civil war of words over America's heart and soul.

For many people, these challenges appear to be overwhelming and beyond their control. As a result, they feel frustrated and helpless. Whether I am conversing with my seatmates on a plane or having dinner with friends, they often share how worried sick they are about what is happening to our country and then throw up their hands and say, "I wish I could do something about it, but no one in Washington is listening."

A beacon of hope for our nation

My response to them is this: "You may be right about Washington, but my experience tells a very different story when it comes to your ability to have a voice and make a difference. In the world in which I work, the vast majority of citizens who comprise our school districts are people like you who are tired of the political infighting and are willing to step up and do the right thing for our children."

Most people who listen to my little "motivational speech" are both surprised and relieved to hear that the American spirit is alive and well. One man, who I believe speaks for many others, commented, "If this can happen in our schools and communities, there is still hope for our country."

As I have chronicled in this and previous chapters, my work with our public schools is filled with stories in which citizens have put aside their parochial concerns and risen to the occasion to meet the educational needs of the children in their communities. If given a chance, we will do the same for our country by tapping into the good that Alexis de Tocqueville discovered when he visited here in 1831.

References

Eisenhower, Dwight D. 1952. Great Books Online. http://www.bartleby.com/73/829.html.

O'Callaghan, William. 1999. *The Power of Public Engagement: A Beacon of Hope for America's Schools*. Manhattan, KS: The MASTER Teacher, Inc.

Rasmussen Reports. 2014, July 9. "Right Direction or Wrong Track." *Rasmussen Reports*. http://www.rasmussenreports.com/public_content/politics/mood_of_america/right_direction_or_wrong_track.

Join the Conversation at
WWW.CorkyOCallaghan.com

Reading this book is the prelude to a much needed national conversation about the future of our education system. In Chapter 19, I discussed what you and a few of your friends can do as thoughtful, committed citizens to help initiate this vitally important discussion.

To support your call to action, I have created a website:

www.CorkyOCallaghan.com

This website is designed to serve as a forum to report on and discuss the progress being made to bring people together to make a difference for our nation's public schools and the communities they serve.

America's schools are at a turning point. Don't wait. Join the conversation now to help shape their future.

Thank you for your support.

Corky O'Callaghan

Appendix

Book Discussion Questions

In writing this book, I had three goals. One was to sound the alarm about how our country's education reform movement is currently impacting our students, teachers, and communities and that, as a result, America's schools are at a turning point. The second was to demonstrate how, in my experience, the American people have nearly always risen to the occasion when the educational needs of their children were at stake and that they will do it again once they become aware of what is happening to their schools. My third goal was to lay out specifically in chapter 19 what we can do as individual citizens to help shape the future of our schools as we move beyond the turning point now facing us. One of the strategies that can be used to get things moving forward is to organize a book study group to read and discuss this book. To help facilitate the conversations, I have created the following discussion questions:

General questions about this book

- What prompted you to read this book?
- What is your main takeaway from the book?
- What in it has surprised you?
- What has given you the most concern?

- If you were to recommend this book to someone else, what would you tell the person?
- Having read this book, what do you believe is the single greatest challenge facing our nation's public schools? Why do you feel this way?

Part I—How We Reached This Point

America's public schools did not reach what is now a pivotal turning point overnight. It has taken place gradually. For over a century, our government has been increasing the burden being placed upon our schools to meet the changing needs and expectations of our society.

- Do you think that our public schools are trying to do too much to address the growing needs of our society? If yes, why? If no, why not?
- What is your opinion regarding school choice?
- How do you feel about high-stakes testing of our students?
- If you had a chance to speak with the teachers in your school district about the Common Core Standards, what would you ask them?
- What most concerns you about the corporate takeover of our nation's public schools?
- What kind of a job do you think our schools are doing to educate our children?

Part II—The Impact of Education Reform

Good intentions can have unintended consequences. While the education reform movement may have been built upon a foundation of good intentions, the unintended consequences of education reform are creating a number of serious challenges that need to be discussed and addressed by the American people.

- On a scale of 1 to 5, with 1 being the lowest and 5 being the highest, how would you rate your level of concern regarding the over-testing of our school children? Why do you feel this way?
- Has over-testing of our students affected your family or any families that you know? If yes, what has been the impact?
- On a scale of 1 to 5, with 1 being not very concerned and 5 being extremely concerned, how concerned are you that our teachers are being overwhelmed by the impact of the education reforms being mandated by our state and federal policymakers? Why do you feel this way?
- Have you had a chance to talk with any teachers you know about how these education reforms are affecting them? If yes, what did they tell you?
- This section of the book also addresses the fact that our nation's education reform movement is undermining support for our schools, dividing our communities, increasing our financial burden, and usurping our responsibility as citizens. On a scale of 1 to 5, with 1 being not very important and 5 being extremely important, how would you rate each of these concerns? Why do you feel this way?

Part III—Missing from Our National Discussion

Two things are missing from our national discussion about education reform. One is the involvement and voice of reason of the American people—the majority of whom care less about politics and more about doing what is best for our children. The other is the willingness of most school superintendents to step up to the plate and explain how the education reform movement is impacting our schools.

- What lesson was learned from the failed attempt by Cory

Booker and Chris Christie to reform the public schools in Newark, New Jersey?

- Why is it important for the voice of the American people to be clearly heard in our nation's discussion about education reform?
- What will it take to free up our voices?
- What can we personally do to encourage our own superintendent of schools to help lead a frank and open district-wide conversation about the impact of education reform on our school system and community?

Part IV—Reason for Hope

Whether it has involved responding to a natural disaster, a threat to our national security, or the educational needs of our children, the American people have always come through when they clearly understood why they were needed. When they realize that our public schools are at a turning point, they will rise to the occasion once again.

- In the stories about how school district residents have come together to successfully address the educational needs of their children, what gives you reason for hope?
- What personal experiences can you share in which your neighborhood, school district, or community worked together to solve a problem?
- Margaret Mead's quote ["Never doubt that a small group of thoughtful, committed citizens can change the world. Indeed, it is the only thing that ever has."] illustrates how book discussions like this one can make a significant difference. How is her quote supported by the Hundredth Monkey story and tipping point research in chapter 17?
- What factors have set the stage for the American people

to get involved in helping shape the future of our nation's schools?

Part V—Where We Go from Here

Today, a growing a growing number of school superintendents are beginning to step up to the plate and sound the alarm that our nation's public schools are at a turning point. There also is evidence that the American people are ready to get involved and make a difference when they are provided with a little guidance on what they can do and how they can do it.

- What is your reaction to the initial attempts by school superintendents to sound the alarm about how our nation's education reform movement is impacting our public schools?
- What do you think of the approach discussed in chapter 19 about how to let your elected representatives know that you want to help them shape the future of our schools?
- Following this book discussion, what ideas do you have for expanding it to include more community members?
- How is the information in this book a beacon of hope for our country?

Acknowledgements

In many respects, this is my favorite section of this book because it serves as an opportunity for me to acknowledge the many people who have helped put me into a position to write it. Since I have a lot of people to thank, let me begin.

Since much of what a person learns is learned early in life, I am going start with my mother and father who are now deceased. If it were not for them, there is a good chance I would never have been able to attend Ohio University and graduate from its School of Journalism with the ability to put my thoughts into words. Another person to whom I am indebted and whose wisdom inspires me every day of my life is my close friend and mentor, Jerry Bell. While Jerry died several years ago in a tragic airplane crash, his common-sense way of identifying what really matters continues to shape how I think.

For the past two decades, my best critic and supporter has been the love of my life, my wife, Diane. Like Jerry had when he was alive, she has the unique ability to cut through all of the diversionary minutia and focus on what is most important. With regard to this book, Diane was my go-to editor—reading every line on every page and letting me know when I needed to make changes.

Throughout my career working with the public schools, a

number of caring individuals took me under their wings and gave me an opportunity to do my thing. My first break came when Dick Maxwell, then county superintendent of schools in Holmes County, Ohio, invited me to meet with his two local superintendents. As a result of that meeting, two career-changing events occurred. One is that I began working with West Holmes Superintendent Dean Werstler who, as I noted in chapter 15, helped create the major turning point in my career. What we accomplished together there continues to be my standard for how the American people need to be treated. The second result of Dick's meeting was that not long afterwards he became the executive director of the Buckeye Association of School Administrators, which is Ohio's statewide superintendent organization, and invited me to conduct workshops on how to pass school tax issues. Today, thanks to the support of his predecessors, Jerry Klenke and Kirk Hamilton, I am still conducting workshops for BASA and working with the association in other ways.

In addition to Dick, Dean, Jerry, and Kirk, I owe a special debt of gratitude to Charlie Irish, Paul Pendleton, Bob Kreiner, Dallas Jackson, Bob Scott, Mike Zalar, Brad Neavin, Greg Ring, Pam Hood, and Steve Barrett. All are current or former Ohio superintendents who have given me a chance to work with them and their school districts and have provided me with the credibility I needed to launch and sustain my consulting career. Following their retirement from the school superintendency, Charlie, Paul, and I formed the Santa Rita Collaborative so we could continue working together. In addition to the aforementioned individuals, I want to acknowledge one more person. Jim Betts and I met several years ago when he was candidate for lieutenant governor of Ohio, and I was helping him raise money to fund the campaign. The friendship we established has endured over the years, and I am eternally grateful for it.

As result of the growing success we were having in passing school tax issues in Ohio, several of my superintendent colleagues and I decided we needed to capture the insights behind these success stories and share them in a book. Thanks to the support of my close friend and future coauthor, Harry Eastridge, and the initial introduction by Scott Howard to the founders and owners of The Master Teacher, Inc., Bob and Tracey DeBruyn took a leap of faith and gave me another big break in my career by publishing *The Power of Public Engagement: A Beacon of Hope for America's Schools*. Bob and Tracey continued their support of our work and published a second book coauthored by Harry and me titled *When the Choir Began to Sing: A Story About Awakening the Leader within Each of Us*.

In 2001, Diane and I decided to build a home in Green Valley, Arizona, a small community about twenty miles south of Tucson. Since retirement was not and continues not to be in my future, I began networking with Arizona's education leaders so I could establish myself in a state where nobody knew me. My first break in Arizona came when Harold Porter, then executive director of the Arizona School Administrators, took me by the hand and introduced me to Arizona's school superintendents. Harold's successors, Roger Short and Debra Duvall, have also been instrumental in supporting me and my work, and I am most appreciative of it. As a result of their support, a number of superintendents have stepped up and given me a chance to work with them. I am especially indebted to Calvin Baker, John Pedicone, Dudley Butts, Vicki Balentine, Manny Valenzuela, Richard Rundhaug, and Robin Berry for their continuing friendship and support. I also want to thank John Gordon, a former superintendent of schools and director of leadership development with the Arizona School Boards Association, and Susan Carlson, recently retired executive director of the Arizona Business and Education Coalition, for giving me an opportunity to work with them and their associations.

Before acknowledging the individuals who have helped edit this book, I would like to thank Jamie Vollmer for the conversations we have had about the state of our nation's public schools. His national perspective has been invaluable in helping to assure that what I have written resonates with what is happening in school districts across our nation. In addition, I want to thank Dave Moore who introduced me to the Kettering Foundation and to acknowledge and thank the Kettering Foundation's David Mathews and Randy Nielsen for helping me to think differently about my work.

In drafting the manuscript for this book, I have turned to two groups of people for help. I have relied upon professional educators and those closely associated with the work of our public schools to help assure that what I am saying in the book resonates with what they know to be accurate and true. They include: long-time friend, colleague, and school board member, Chris Long; teachers and husband and wife, Tom and Janet Hackley; a teacher and my sister-in-law, Karen Muldowney; Arizona charter school teacher, Lori Malangone; former superintendent and now assistant professor of education at the University of Arizona, Vicki Balentine; and current superintendents Jeff Langdon, Greg Ring, Bob Scott, Bob Hill, Brad Neavin, Steve Barrett, Jay Arbaugh, Manny Valenzuela, Mike Paskewicz, Rocky Killion, Mike Zalar, and Pam Hood.

In addition to my wife, I have relied upon two individuals who have no connection to what is happening in our public schools to help assure that the book's content flows smoothly and is clear. They are my sister-in-law, Anita Woodward, and my friend and Arizona neighbor, Michele Lewis.

If I have forgotten to mention anyone, and there is a good chance that I have, I would like to apologize to them right now. Over the years, I have received so much help from so many people that it is hard to remember everyone. I am truly blessed.

The Author

William G. "Corky" O'Callaghan has spent the past twenty-five years helping educational leaders utilize the power of community engagement to build public support for placing tax issues on the ballot, restructuring educational programs and services, and addressing other challenges and opportunities impacting their schools and community.

He has worked in more than three hundred school districts throughout Ohio and a number of districts and educational organizations in Arizona which include the Arizona School Boards Association, the Arizona School Administrators, and the Arizona Business and Education Coalition.

He is author of *The Power of Public Engagement: A Beacon of Hope for America's Schools, Putting the Power of Public Engagement to Work for Your Schools and Community* and *Thinking Outside the Box: How Educational Leaders Can Safely Navigate the Rough Waters of Change.* He also coauthored *When the Choir Began to Sing: A Story about Awakening the Leader Who Lives Within Each of Us.*

In 1995, he founded the Mohican Institute, a think tank for Ohio's school superintendents, and, in 2005, he received the Distinguished Service Award from the Buckeye Association of School

Administrators in recognition of his outstanding service to education in Ohio.

He and his wife, Diane, reside in Cleveland, Ohio, and Green Valley, Arizona.

CPSIA information can be obtained at www.ICGtesting.com
Printed in the USA
BVOW07s1919271014

372554BV00002B/53/P